To
In loving memory

who cared enough to help

me discover the real me

Cover art by Annette Lewis. In her own words:

Art has always been a part of my life. As a child, art was my favorite thing to do. My first memory is one of finger painting up to my elbows. My family always encouraged me to draw and paint. As an adult, following three years of art school, I went into the field of advertising. Ten years of graphic art work (first for a newspaper and then for an advertising agency) led to my current work of teaching art classes- both group and private lessons.

I have always loved creating art: pencil drawings, watercolor, pastels, murals, keepsake jewelry, sculpture, etc. It provides me with a feeling of freedom in being able to express myself, as well as a sense of accomplishment that I can make others happy with my work. As I appreciate the art in life all around me, I feel it is God's way of inspiring me to be creative. Because I get great pleasure from a variety of media, it is rewarding to share that enjoyment with the children in my classes.

Having the opportunity to do the cover art for this book has been an honor and a blessing for me and has led to other book illustration projects, for which I am truly excited and thankful.

You may contact Annette at: **dallasrober@aol.com**

Table of Contents

Foreword By Cathy Lee Phillips
Page xi

Acknowledgments
Page xiii

Introduction
Page xvii

PART ONE
Who the Heck is Debi Merchant?
Page 1

Chapter 1
Paradox R Me
Page 3

Chapter 2
And the Valedictorian for the Class of 1971 is...
NOT Debbie Barrington
Page 9

Chapter 3
The Deacon's Daughter
Page 15

Chapter 4
Debisms
Page 19

Chapter 5
Divorced and Surviving Single
Page 25

Chapter 6
With This Ring
Page 29

PART TWO
Relationships
It's All Relative....Usually
Page 35

Chapter 1
Beck's Bad Girl
Page 37

Chapter 2
Not by Blood
Page 43

Chapter 3
My Tribute
Page 47

Chapter 4
Siblings – Just Because I Wasn't One Doesn't Mean I'm Not One
Page 51

Chapter 5
All My Children
Page 55

Chapter 6
Happy Holidays!
Page 61

Chapter 7
The Grand Entrances!
Page 65

Chapter 8
Others Swimming in My Gene Pool (Their Fingerprints are on My Life)
Page 73

Chapter 9
The Blues Sisters
Page 81

PART THREE
Dancing Like No One's Watching
Page 85

Chapter 1
Always Look to Make Sure There
Isn't a Frog in Your Toilet
Page 87

Chapter 2
To Thine Own Self Be True –
I'm Working on It
Page 89

Chapter 3
Who's In Charge?
Page 93

Chapter 4
Life's a Baseball Game –
Swing That Bat!
Page 97

Chapter 5
Is This The Number To Whom I'm Speaking?
Page 101

Chapter 6
Through Their Eyes
Page 105

Chapter 7
No Time Like the Present
Page 109

Chapter 8
Pray Without Ceasing
Page 113

Chapter 9
You Can't Judge a Book by Its Cover
Page 115

Chapter 10
Four P's in 2007's Pod
Page 119

Chapter 11
Where I've Been, Where I Am, Where I'm Going
Page 123

About the Author
Page 131

Contact Information
Page 133

Foreword

Debi with an "i" never wanted to be like everyone else. Trust me. She isn't. She changed her name to avoid being the owner of the more traditional spelling, D E B B I E. Debi Merchant most certainly dances her own dance, sings her own song, and now even writes her own book!

Debi is quite a character. No! Debbie is actually a whole *cast* of characters – wife, mother, daughter, sister, grandmother, (she will happily show you several hundred photos of her latest grandchild born just a few weeks ago), a died-in-the-wool southerner, the deacon's daughter, and the non-valedictorian of her 1971 high school graduating class. Debi is part of a super-sized family and overseer of a collection of animals known as the *zoo crew*. Obviously her garage is quite crowded. No worry. If space gets too tight, Debi will knock out a wall, invite a new group of friends, and keep on dancing.

Of course, hers is not a tangible garage with a concrete floor, two cars, tool boxes, gardening supplies, paint cans, old furniture, and a few fishing rods. This *garage* is a metaphor for Debi's life with its myriad experiences and unique characters. Just like any other garage, Debi's holds a host of memories. Some are joyful while others are frustrating. Some memories are gut-wrenching ones when Debi used every ounce of her faith just to keep moving. Others are pleasing and accompanied by the sound of happy laughter. All are bound by a strong cord of trust in Jesus Christ. It is her trust and faith that enables Debi to keep on dancing.

I met Debi when I led a women's spiritual retreat for her church, Due West United Methodist Church in Marietta, Georgia. As we talked, I was impressed with her obvious desire to embark on a ministry of writing and speaking. It is a calling for her and I can only admire a woman who moves heaven and earth to achieve her dream and to do what God is calling her to do. Debi has taken the wheel and is the driver on her own journey. God, however, is the navigator who points the way.

Join Debi's dance as, in her natural, conversational way, she relates events that have challenged, shaped, and defined her faith. Feel free to laugh out loud at her stories, her characters, and the weird situations she stumbles into. She wants you to learn and laugh with her. Most of all, she wants you to grow in faith with her – always reaching, seeking, and striving to become a more effective disciple of Jesus Christ.

After all, isn't this a goal we all share?

--Cathy Lee Phillips
Atlanta, Georgia
September 2007

Acknowledgments

There are so many people I'd like to thank and I will attempt to do so without leaving anyone out. Here goes:

Thank you, God, for all you have done in my life. Thank you for loving me in spite of all my warts. Thank you for never giving up on me. Thank you for all the blessings you've given me and the opportunity to share my faith journey with others.

Thank you, Karen Ethridge [my cousin] for getting my original WORKS files into a WORD document so that I wouldn't have to re-key the whole manuscript! I was in a major panic until you came to my rescue.

Thanks to all my friends in District 14 of Toastmasters International (with a special shout-out to the North Metro, South Cobb, and Legacy Owl clubs) and the ADI Speakers Workshop. All of you have inspired and encouraged me not only as I've worked on this book but also in my life journey.

Thanks also to my church family at Due West United Methodist Church. Y'all are such an accepting group of people, and you have encouraged me, prayed for me and prayed with me as I have walked with you since 1997.

Thanks to all of my co-workers at the U.S. Government Printing Office (the ones in the Atlanta office as well as all of you in the other GPO offices around the country). Y'all have encouraged me and have helped me to grow as a person and challenged me to live my faith Monday through Friday and not just on Sundays – not preaching it – living it.

Thanks to the many friends I've made since 2001 (the first year I participated in the Breast Cancer 3-Day Walk in Atlanta). The *Silver Comet Trekkers*, the *Scoobyboobs*, fellow crew members on Pit Stop #1 – all of you have meant so much to me and have helped me become a better person.

Thank you, Cathy Lee Phillips, for leading the Due West UMC Women's Retreat in March 2006, and touching my life. You not only inspired me with your words and your life, but you also befriended me and took me under your wings as you guided me in my book-writing adventure.

Thank you Ed Hale, a fellow pilgrim in the Faith Journey for reading one of the earlier manuscripts and suggesting the title for this book.

Thank you Deb Christmas, my partner at the US Government Printing Office and a fellow bookworm. You spent many lunch hours reading and editing my manuscript.

Thank you Annette Lewis, my wonderfully talented friend who's trying desperately to help me find the connection to my "left brain". Your artwork is awesome, and you got right into my head and drew the cover I'd seen in my mind's eye but couldn't put on paper.

Thank you, Pat Veal for encouraging me to be true to myself and to God. With your words of wisdom you have caused me to delve deeper into my beliefs and to tap into the Source of my strength.

Thank you, Mae Pace for being a 2nd *Mama* to me in Hanahan, SC, and for loving me all these years. You give the best hugs ever!

Thank you, Iris and Steve Broadbent for your friendship. Iris, without your love and encouragement I would never have met the real me, and would not have become who I am today. Steve, you are one of the most unpretentious people I know, and I appreciate the spin you put on life because it keeps me honest.

And finally, I want to thank my family. I am humbled to be a part of such a wonderful group of people: My parents, Jerry and Margie Barrington, for your love, support, and acceptance – even when you think I'm a little nuts and perhaps have one or two screws loose; to my sisters Kathy, Gail, and Jo Ellen, for teaching me how to be a sibling – the three of you are the best sisters anyone could have; to my nephews and nieces, Mark, Amy, Julie, Joel, and Kaylin - your love means so much to me; and all my aunts, uncles, and cousins (they are like the stars in the sky – too many to name individually) – but I want all of you to know how much each and every one of you mean to me.

Thank you, Merchant family (Peggy, Sherwood, Mark, Cindy, Melissa, Molly, and Miranda) for accepting and embracing me as a member of your family and for encouraging me all the many years that I've been writing this book.

Thank you, Wes Brown, my son-in-law. You are such a loving husband to Jeri and daddy to Mackenzie and Macyn. You are a wonderful addition to our family, and I'm so glad you became a part of us – even when you realized we were a little (okay, a lot) nuts.

Mackenzie, thank you for loving your Grams and sharing your life with me. Thank you for all the joy you've brought into my life, and for reminding me of the wonder and awe of viewing life through the eyes of a child. Macyn, the newest member of our family, thank you for another opportunity to view life through the eyes of a child. Even though you are only a few weeks old at this writing, my life has already been changed by you, and I'm full of anticipation and excitement as I look forward to getting to know you.

Thanks to my children:

Jeri, thank you for being one of my best friends. You keep me on target and call it like it is when I veer off course. I can always count on you to be honest with me, and help me see things as they really are. Thank you for proofreading and editing an earlier manuscript and helping to get the files into printable form.

James, thank you for your *James hugs* – they always have and always will mean so much to me. Your quick wit and your awesome smile make my day. Thank you for your take on life and for sharing your thoughts and dreams with me. Thank you, too, for keeping me stocked with UGA items even though it pains your *Tennessee Vol's* spirit to do so.

Jena, thank you for allowing me to call you my *daughter*. It means so much for me to be a part of your life. I treasure our relationship and those late night talks we have as we try to solve all the problems of the world. Thank you for challenging me to stay up to date on current events and also for your spin on things which keeps me on my toes.

And finally, thank you, Matthew, my wonderful husband. Without your encouragement and your gently pushing me forward, this book would still be just a dream. Thank you for believing in me. Thank you for cheering me on when I was discouraged. Thank you for understanding me and for putting up with my quirks – basically for loving me *warts and all*. Thank you for all the many times you were left to do most of the day-to-day chores as I worked night after night to complete this manuscript. Thank you for walking with me as we enter this new chapter in our lives, because I know with you by my side, I won't fall far because you will catch me – just like you always do. I love you.

Introduction

One day while cleaning my garage, I decided to turn on some music. As the songs swept through my soul, I really *got into it* as the kids say, and before I knew it I was DANCING IN THE GARAGE! Yes, that's right – dancing from one box to the other, from one corner to the other, from one cob web to the other – dancing all over my garage – sometimes with my broom, sometimes free-style. I'm sure I looked like a fool but, hey, the garage was getting clean, I was getting exercise and I was having fun!

As I continued to dance I had an epiphany. I realized my life was like a garage, containing a wide variety of boxes that I had collected over the years. With the music pulsating through my body, memories emerged and I was transported from my physical garage to the garage of my life. As I danced from one box of my life to the next, I realized I had experienced deep joy as well as deep sorrow. I discovered, however, through it all I had maintained my faith and my sense of humor. Jesus Christ and laughter were common threads throughout the experiences in my life.

Laughter is very healthy and it sure makes life a lot more bearable, especially on the dark days. I'm convinced that Jesus laughed many times but it isn't mentioned in the Bible because He did it all the time. [The reason I know this is because I've never read a verse stating that He went to the restroom – but we all know He did.] So as you dance with me, laughter will be part of the song!

Scripture will also be part of song. Sometimes as I'm going about the business of living, all of a sudden a Scripture pops into my mind that totally fits the moment! I pause, I embrace it and I thank God for it – then I dance. My stories are peppered with an occasional Scripture that popped into my head as I was dancing by that particular box in my garage.

God has always used ordinary people to do His work. And that is who I am – an ordinary person whose life has been touched in many extraordinary ways by God. His love has sustained me in every corner of my garage. He placed other ordinary people on my dance floor as examples, as anchors, as guides for me as the songs changed and as the rhythm required a new dance.

As I danced through my garage, I realized just how special all the various people in my life are, and even though we didn't (and don't) always agree on everything, I appreciate and love each of them dearly. I am so thankful that each has been and continues to be a part of my dance.

Dancing in my garage gave me an appreciation for the past, hope for the future, and contentment in the present.

Dance with me through the garage of my life. Hopefully my experiences will make your journey easier, bring a smile to your face, give you a huge belly laugh, or perhaps just help you think deeply about some things and consider another point of view. If nothing else, just enjoy the afternoon reading…and dancing!

Psalm 149:3 – **Let them praise his name in the dance: let them sing praises unto him with the timbrel and harp.** (KJV)

PART ONE

Who the Heck is Debi Merchant?

You may be wondering who Debi Merchant is. Sometimes I wonder that myself. It seems I'm wired differently than most people, so it's difficult to know exactly what makes me tick, and how on earth I come to some of the conclusions that I do. Hopefully Part One of the book will give you some insights into me. You may even figure me out. [By the way, if you do figure me out, please share that information with my husband – he's been working on that project for years.]

Some of my personal sayings are: If it ain't pork, it ain't BBQ; If it ain't rich and sweet, it ain't dessert; If it ain't caffeinated, it ain't coffee; and If it ain't "Coca-Cola," it ain't "a Coke!" And why would I share those with you? Why not?

Chapter 1
Paradox R Me

Many years ago, Donnie and Marie Osmond performed a song on their TV variety show that really nails my personality. The words said that one of them was a *little bit country* and the other one was a *little bit rock 'n roll*. That's me – not only in my musical tastes, but in all aspects of my life, which explains why I'm also *a little bit nuts*. I am the epitome of the word *paradox*. Mr. Webster must have know someone like me when he defined that word. I'm most likely the most conforming, non-conformist that you will ever meet.

My journey we call life began on February 7, 1953, in Macon, Georgia. I am the only child of Jerry and Robbie Barrington. (In 1973, after my mother died, Dad remarried. Mom's name is Margie and thanks to her, I finally got sisters – overnight! The entire story unfolds in later chapters, so keep dancing.)

I was named Mary Deborah Barrington and was called *Debbie*, spelled D-e-b-b-i-e. As a teenager, I decided that there were just too many D-e-b-b-i-e-s and D-e-b-b-y-s running around – remember the non-conforming thing? So, I decided to change the spelling of my name to D-e-b-i. My mother wouldn't hear of it so I remained D-e-b-b-i-e until I was 30 when it dawned on me I could spell my name any way I wanted and I finally became D-e-b-i.

I have two other nicknames – *Dee* (which I called myself as a small child) and *Snafu*, which is Dad's nickname for me. For years I just thought that was a cute, unusual name. Little did I know it is an Army term that for the purposes of the PG rating of this book means: **S**ituation **N**ormal, **A**ll **F**ouled **U**p! So those who know me well have my dad to thank for all the times you are scratching your heads wondering what in the world I am thinking. [See Chapter 4 – *Debisms*.]

We lived in a two-bedroom, one bath, house where I shared a room with my maternal grandmother (Mommy Steppe). I remember a friend telling me that she thought we were rich (we weren't) because we lived in a brick house. I thought we were rich the day we got a window air-conditioner. We weren't.

My childhood was rather uneventful unless, of course, you count two major surgeries that came close to ending my journey of life. The fact that I survived both of them has always led me to believe that God has a special plan for me. He and I are still working out the details.

My reaction to the second surgery set the stage for the way I react to most situations. As they were rolling me to the operating room, I recited the following Bible verse over and over again: **What time I am afraid, I will trust in thee.** Psalm 56:3 (KJV). I was seven years old and had just learned that verse in Sunday school. I was scared to death so I decided to trust God and hold Him to His Word. He didn't fail me then, and He has never failed me since.

In 1964 the U.S. Government closed several facilities. My parents worked at one of them so we transferred from the Macon area to Charleston, SC. We bought a house in Hanahan, about ten miles north of Charleston. That house was a three-bedroom house but still only had one bathroom. It amazes me that today we all think we have to have at least two baths...on each floor. I thought we were really uptown because we had a carport. Hanahan was the epitome of the *bedroom* community of that day and life was good.

As I got older, I hated being an only child. I also hated doing dishes, so sometimes (okay, usually) I'd get out clean dishes to wash along with the dirty ones to pretend that I had a large family. Talk about an overactive imagination! However, my imagination is where I grew up. That's where I became me. My *world in a box* as I call it is where I learned to run things through my filters and began to formulate my beliefs. That's also probably the reason I'm wired differently than most people. In my *world in a box* no one ever questioned my thought processes so, consequently, I grew up thinking the whole world viewed things pretty much the way I did – only to find out that that is not always (okay, almost never) the case. Oh well, I am uniquely and wonderfully made. It says so in the Bible. **I will praise thee; for I am fearfully and wonderfully made:** Psalm 139:14a (KJV). But I digress again, back to the story...

My imagination is also where I hid so that I wouldn't hurt so badly when life threw me those curves that are part of all our lives.

In my thirties I began to think that because of my imaginary world, I had missed out on real life since I had been so busy imagining this or that. However, I've come to understand that I am who I am because many times when I couldn't voice aloud what I felt, my *world in a box* accepted me and I felt enough self worth to continue to function day to day. For so many years the true *me* was far beneath the surface. I spent the first twenty years of my life trying to please my mother, who tried her best to make me someone that I was not. It's almost as if those first twenty years were lived in a cocoon.

After my mother died and as I moved through my twenties, the cocoon began to open little by little. By the time I was in my thirties the butterfly emerged and began to fly. That is why a beautiful blue butterfly adorns my left ankle. It is there to remind me where I've been and to guide me where I'm headed.

I was brought up in a very conservative Christian home and I became VERY pious. I was *so* pious the class prophet of my graduating class prophesied, "Debbie Barrington has just returned from her fourth worldwide tour with Billy Graham and she is retranslating the Bible due to some discrepancies she found."

I never realized it until I began writing this book, but the class prophet might have been onto something. My interpretation of the Scripture is much different now than it was then. I've come to realize that there is not just one interpretation of the Scripture. God is so wonderful! He inspired the writers of the Scripture in such a way that the verses speak to each of us individually. The Scripture speaks to us where we are at any given moment in our life's journey allowing the Holy Spirit to work in us in different ways on different days in different times of our life.

It's not up to me to be a judge of anyone and I refuse to accept that position. I just know what is right for me, based on my relationship with God. I don't pretend to be someone I'm not – what you see IS what you get and sometimes what you get isn't pretty. I make more than my share of mistakes on a daily basis and have to ask forgiveness. Who am I to judge someone else?

Occasionally, I follow my heart instead of my head. All of a sudden, I'll find myself in a weird or uncomfortable situation that's totally not where I thought I was headed.

My head says, "How the heck did we get here?"

My heart replies, "I'm not sure, but I'll get us out of here somehow."

Now, since my heart is not a man, it will ask for directions when necessary, and usually we're able to get all the body parts working together and get out of the dilemma…usually. There are those extreme circumstances which require a lot of sweating and wringing of the hands before things get better, but they always work out one way or another and usually with no casualties.

I march to a different drummer, but at least I march. Here are a few things that keep me marching: 1) my faith; 2) my sense of humor; 3) my sense of wonderment; 4) my zest for life; 5) a full cell battery for my phone; 6) something in the freezer I can throw together to eat when friends drop by unexpectedly; 7) a hidden key in case I lock myself out (again); and 8) my ability to sing along with the radio at the top of my lungs no matter who is listening.

Through it all, my life has been and continues to be a combination of liberal vs. conservative views, many shades of gray, and very few distinct black or white areas. However, the one thing that I'm SURE of – the one area of my life where there is NO ROOM for negotiation – is my personal relationship with Jesus Christ. As I grow and change, my relationship with Christ remains intact. Jesus

Christ is the center of my life and the defining piece of the puzzle to the paradox of Debi Merchant.

I can't explain how I got to where I am today other than to say that in all the years of living in *my world in a box*, the one true constant in my life has been God. No matter what was happening around me, all I had to do was plug into my Source of Strength – and I did so over and over again. I learned very early that my relationship with God is the one thing that I can always count on to see me through every situation.

He will do for you what He has done for me. Tap into His strength and find the Power that you need.

John 14:18 – **I will not leave you comfortless: I will come to you.** (KJV)

Chapter 2
And the Valedictorian for the Class of 1971 is...NOT Debbie Barrington

One of the biggest disappointments of my life occurred on June 3, 1971 – the night I graduated from Hanahan High School.

I had been on the honor roll the entire 12 years I'd been in school. Mother insisted on it. There was only one time that I received less than an A. I made one B+ in Geography in the 7th grade.

I will never forget the day I opened my report card and saw that B+ in Geography. I knew it was the end of my life as I knew it. Mother would kill me once I got home. Thank goodness we received our report cards at the end of the day because I would not have been able to function at all that day if we'd received them earlier. It was all I could do to gather my things, get my bike out of the rack and ride home.

I didn't know then, nor do I know now, how I got a B+ without seeing it coming. One of the great mysteries in my life is why I didn't ask the teacher what happened. Looking back now, that would have been such a simple thing to do. But that is not who I was back then and for some reason it never occurred to me to ask what happened. Given that I was programmed to be grade oriented, one would think I would have known my Geography grade wasn't where it needed to be. I can honestly say I had no clue and was a wreck the rest of the afternoon.

Mother knew it was Report Card Day, so of course the first thing she wanted to do when she arrived home from work was to see my report card. Even as I write this 41 years later, my mouth is dry and my stomach is tightening. I see the 7th grade version of myself swallowing hard, choking back tears and handing Mother the card with a trembling hand. I see me holding my breath and realize I'm holding my breath now. I see the moment, as I did on that afternoon, when she zeroes in on the B+. I see me cringe as she begins her tirade and I cringe now. A chill goes down my spine and I try to shake it off.

Dad came to my rescue that afternoon. He took the report card, averaged all six grades and told Mother that my overall average was in the A+ (95-100) range – still the *Principal's Honor Roll*. I let out a slow, low breath now as I did then waiting for Mother's response. Mother stopped yelling. WHEW! Saved by Daddy. I would live another day. (Actually, I did receive a few B's in one more subject during 8th grade – Physical Education; but Mother didn't consider that to be a *real subject*, so there was no fury.)

In Hanahan, 1st through 7th grades were elementary school and 8th through 12th grades were high school. There were two elementary schools that fed into the one high school. I was the top honor graduate of Hanahan Elementary School and I made it my goal to be the top honor graduate of Hanahan High School. I set my plan in motion.

I studied. I did extra credit assignments. I turned in all my work on time. I kept a running tally of all my grades – all the things an honor student does. [I didn't realize it at the time, but these habits gave birth to my work ethic, and that has served me well during my career.]

All of my courses were college prep courses, at least until my senior year. At some point during my junior year in high school my *world in a box* crashed and burst open at my feet and I decided I would not attend college. As I reflect back trying to remember exactly why I made that decision, it's difficult to narrow it down to one thing. Many things going on in my life at that time contributed to that decision. I'm not sure which ones carried more weight:

#1 – Mother made the announcement that due to the deaths at Kent State, I would not be living on campus anywhere. Since I had my heart set on the University of Georgia and we lived in Hanahan, SC, that pretty much squashed that dream.

#2 – I was tired. Tired of always studying. I had come to the realization that I didn't possess above average intelligence because the grades did not come easily. I studied long and hard to maintain them and I knew Mother would insist on Dean's List in college and I wasn't at all sure I could deliver. My head felt it would explode as I continued to fill it with facts, figures, dates. I was suffering from burn out and didn't know it.

#3 - Money. In order to afford college, I needed scholarships. In order to qualify for scholarships, I needed high grades and a high SAT score. It never occurred to me to discuss my concerns with the guidance counselor at school. I know she would have helped me work through all of the confusion, the stress, the process and, who knows, maybe my life would have taken a different course. But then, there would be no Chapter 2 in this book. Very likely, there would be no book at all...

Rather than load my class schedule during my senior year with Calculus, Advanced Comp, and other such courses, I took the two courses I needed to complete the college prep requirements (should I ever decide to attend college). I also took two business courses (in order to begin working after graduation) and two study halls (to rest).

On the first day of class, the guidance counselor sought me out and asked me to come to her office. She put her arms around my shoulders as we made the trip down the hall. She closed the door, offered me a chair in front of her desk, sat in another chair and leaned in close as she said, "Debbie, I'm going to share something with you that I shouldn't. You have the highest grade average in the school and no one can catch you. However, you will not be the Valedictorian of your class unless you drop the business courses and take two more college prep courses."

"What if I get 100 averages in both of the business courses?" I asked (because that was my plan).

"It won't matter. The school will not award Valedictorian to a business student." She had no idea everything else churning around in my head and in my life because, as I stated earlier, I never told her. I was very stubborn, though, and decided I would prove her wrong. I saw the disappointment mixed with compassion in her eyes. I thanked her for caring, we hugged, and I left her office convinced I would prevail as Valedictorian of the Class of 1971. She watched me walk down the hall knowing that I would not.

Even though I knew I wasn't any smarter than anyone else, my peers considered me to be a *brain*, which was confirmed as I received the coveted Senior Superlative of *Most Intellectual*. Not *Best All Around, Best Dressed, Best Looking, Most Likely to Succeed, Wittiest*...no, I was *Most Intellectual*. I envisioned a picture of my male counterpart and me being superimposed into a shelf of library books for the yearbook shot because that's how the *Most Intellectual* pair from Dad's graduating class were depicted in his yearbook. I was mortified! Oh well, if that was the price to pay to be valedictorian, so be it.

Senior year passed quickly and it was by far the most exciting year I ever experienced in school. My overall average was 98.6 and I was convinced I had proven the guidance counselor wrong. As graduation day approached, the top honor graduates were asked to prepare speeches for the big night, and I busily began working on my speech. I was flying high knowing my name would go down in the history books of Hanahan as the '71 Valedictorian and I was secretly hoping someone would announce that I'd made Honor Roll for 12 years.

The night began with all of the graduates arriving early to line up. *Pomp and Circumstance* played as we processed into the auditorium and took our places on the stage. As one of the top honor graduates, I was sitting on the first row.

All of the speeches were given, all of the scholarships (except two) were awarded, and then came the moment I'd been waiting for the past five years – the moment the Valedictorian was announced! I was preparing to look surprised – like Miss America and Miss Universe on TV, but my name was not called. I was stunned. I'm sure my mouth fell open as I tried to retain my composure. I remember thinking "that's okay, that's okay, I'll be Salutatorian," but then that honor was bestowed and again, my name was not called. I felt light-headed and nauseous. The guidance counselor's words came rushing back to me like a freight train out of control. I wanted to run from the stage, I wanted to crawl in a hole somewhere. But neither was in my bag of options so I willed myself to stay in my seat, not faint and to ultimately receive my diploma. I had missed the mark. I had not listened to wise counsel. I had disappointed myself.

Fast forward 21 years. In 1992, the classes of '71, '72, and '73 had a combined reunion. One of my classmates introduced me to his wife as our Valedictorian. Go figure! In the scheme of life, does it matter that I wasn't the Valedictorian? No, it doesn't. I did learn some valuable lessons:

Listen to wise counsel;

Don't get cocky in your assessment of yourself;

Stay focused on your goal;

Failing to attain a goal doesn't make you a failure;

Even though you may not attain a goal, God will still bless your life.

As we journey through life there are many times we will set goals we fail to reach. We must learn from those experiences and become better and stronger. We must share our lessons with others, thereby contributing to the growth of our fellow travelers – Debi Barrington Merchant, NOT the Valedictorian of '71.

Chapter 3
The Deacon's Daughter

I am *the deacon's daughter* and I must say that at age 54 I'm very proud of that distinction – although that has not always been the case. No, there were times when I was told that I couldn't do this or that because, "You're the deacon's daughter," and I thought it was the biggest curse ever.

One of those times sticks my memory banks like no other. Let's dance by that box and take a peek: It was the spring of 1971 and my senior in high school. I was the pianist and the preacher's daughter, one of my best friends, was the organist at our church. She was a junior but was dating a senior. I won't bore you with all the details, but let's just say that the prom fell during revival week at our church. Did I mention that I was a senior? It was my *senior prom*. Long story short, the preacher's daughter went to the prom (did I mention that she was a JUNIOR?) and the deacon's daughter went to revival and played the piano. I know, I know, it's been 36 years – let it go. I have, really, I have. I'm just explaining why I hated the term *deacon's daughter* for so many years. Let's dance on.

One of my favorite childhood memories is our annual kite flying adventure. Neither of us was any good at flying kites but every spring the two of us would head out to buy the perfect kite. We'd come home and create the perfect tail using an old sheet. I can still hear the sound of the sheet tearing as Dad pulled the strips apart. We'd hook up all the strips onto the kite string carefully weaving it just so, and then we'd head outside with our masterpiece that we both KNEW was the best kite EVER. We'd run like wild people through the yard with the kite trailing behind us. It would get some lift and begin to ascend into the heavens and then after about two seconds it would promptly crash into a million pieces. We'd look at each other like two scientists in a lab, scratch our heads, pick up all the pieces and go back into the house to repair the kite so that we could start the process all over again. Ah, the memory brings a smile and sense of pure innocent pleasure that I don't experience nearly often enough...

Dad and I love to disagree on a number of things just for the heck of it. We've always loved to argue with one another about everything, especially politics and religion. We have locked horns and butted heads for as long as I can remember but through it all our love for one another, as well as our relationship, has remained strong. Good grief, it just occurred to me as I was writing this paragraph that my dad is truly a genius. What better way to prepare a child to support his or her beliefs than encourage the child to support those beliefs in a good homespun argument. I'm speechless (well, almost).

During my teen years Dad and I fought about many things, but part of that was because we were so much alike. While he won't admit it, I inherited my stubborn streak from him. Through all the shouting matches, through all the disagreements, I always respected him – even when I didn't show it. Because of the relationship we've always had, I know I can be completely honest with Daddy. He accepts me for who I am and he loves me unconditionally, which is the only way my dad knows how to love. My relationship with God would not be what it is today had I not had a dad that lived a life that showed me that I could trust my Heavenly Father.

One of my most prized possessions from Dad is his old Bible that he gave me years ago. I remember him using it when I was a child. Somewhere along the line he got a new Bible and I asked if I could have the old one. The youth group Gonzalez Baptist Church gave him the Bible on September 17, 1946 – way before highlighters were invented. Dad used a red pencil to shade verses that were important to him. He also wrote notes on some of the pages, and not only do I get a glimpse of God as I read this Bible, I also get a glimpse of Dad and what he was thinking all those years ago.

If I had to state the one thing besides his faith in God that my Dad has taught me, it would be not to take myself too seriously – and he didn't verbalize that to me; he lived it.

About a week after Mother died, it was time for a young trainee in my Dad's office to go back home to Pennsylvania. She'd been down South for about six months and the office gave her a going away party. Dad hadn't returned to work yet but decided to go in for her party. The office had taken up a collection to purchase her a nice gift but as she finished opening it, Dad walked up to her with a smaller gift in his hand and a twinkle in his eye. She broke out laughing as she opened her box of grits! Later she told Dad she was surprised that he was able to joke around so soon after losing his wife. My Dad's reply sums up how he lives his life, "I keep laughing so I won't cry." Without saying it in words, Dad lived my mantra – how we respond to our circumstances is our choice.

The most amazing story about Dad is that a very long time ago in Macon, GA, he taught a young boy in Sunday School by the name of Hubert. Hubert grew up and became a Minister of Music in Macon, GA. He had a young boy in his youth choir by the name of Eddie, who grew up to be a Minister of Music in Powder Springs, GA. Eddie had a young girl in his youth choir by the name of Jeri (my daughter) – which goes to prove that what you sow for the Lord does come back to you.

Galatians 6:9 – **And let us not be weary in well doing: for in due season we shall reap, if we faint not.** (KJV)

I am so proud to be *the deacon's daughter*. I would not be the person I am today without Dad's influence in my life. Through all the ups and downs of my life, on all the roads that I've traveled, my faith has sustained me. And that faith began with a little girl, *the deacon's daughter*, watching her Daddy live his faith day in and day out.

Ephesians 6:4 – **Fathers, do not exasperate your children; instead, bring them up in the training and instruction of the Lord.** (NIV)

Chapter 4
Debisms

During most of my early years, I was told I didn't have any common sense. When people tell you something long enough you may begin to believe it. The fact that my common sense didn't kick in right away on many occasions didn't mean I had none, but the fact I was constantly teased about it made it even slower to kick in.

I tend to learn things the hard way. Like, don't remove food from the microwave without gloves. I do understand the dish will be hot. But like the dog who begs at the supper table for a bite of food even though he's never been fed from the table a day in his life, I think the day will come when I'll be fast enough to move the dish from the microwave to the table without burning myself.

The kitchen is a dangerous room for me. Something I've done more than once (you'd think I'd learn) is trying to clean my gas stove at the same time that I'm trying to cook. Yeah, you guessed it. I'll get in a hurry and pick up the pan from the burner I just turned off and move it to another, and then proceed to pick up the HOT burner to clean. The key work is *burn*er because I burn every finger on my hand!

Stuff like this happens all the time. I've just reconciled myself to the fact that this is who I am. I've come to refer to these experiences as "Debisms."

I've spent the better part of my life entertaining people without even trying. I either hear something wrong and make a comment based on what I thought I heard, or I DO something totally innocent that has everyone who sees it dying laughing. And I'm standing there wondering, "What's so funny?"

I'm not sure exactly when the "Debisms" began but as I think back, the first time I remember doing something that could be put in that category occurred in the early 1960's. As my family was seated in a restaurant waiting for the waitress to come with the menus, I looked around at all the pictures on the wall. One of the hangings wasn't a picture, but a sign that read "We reserve the right to refuse service to anyone." I sized up the place, decided that we were in the area that would be considered *the right* [side] and told Dad we'd better move to a table on the left because this section was reserved for refusing service to people! He and Mother almost fell out of their chairs laughing, but I was dead serious! I could just envision us sitting there forever while they refused service to us.

One would hope I'd outgrow the tendency to make a complete fool of myself, but it followed me into adulthood. I began working at the Naval Base in Charleston when I was 18. One day, a sailor came in and asked where the head was. I sent him to my boss's office. OOPS! The *head* is a slang term for restroom in Navy jargon. Who knew? Another day, a customer asked if we had a stevedore. I told them that no STEVE ADORE worked there. How was I to know that a stevedore is someone who is responsible for loading and unloading ships?

My sister Jo Ellen went with me to the mall one day when Jeri was about a year old. I parked in the last spot available at the end of the lane. Once we finished shopping, we walked the fifty miles back to the car, only to find out the parking lot had begun to fill up. The spot directly in front of us was vacant and, not wanting to chance backing into someone (backing has never been my strong suit – hence the bent gate posts at Dad's house), I decided to drive forward. I didn't realize the planter box at the end of the parking lane was jutting into my parking space, but as I rolled forward my right front wheel went up and over the planter box, but the back wheel didn't have enough traction to do so. Uh-oh! I couldn't move backward or forward. I got out of the car to assess the situation while Jo Ellen sat laughing hysterically in the front seat holding Jeri (this just may rank as my all time #1 "Debism"). After realizing my car was virtually sitting on top of the planter box and I couldn't get it off, we walked the fifty miles back to the mall to use a pay phone to call my husband. I was hoping he'd offer to come help me. Instead, he told me to tell Jo Ellen to keep Jeri in the mall and for me to return alone to the car to rock it back and forth until I had enough traction to make the wheels go up and over the planter box. When I asked where the gas tank was – at least I was smart enough to realize all that rocking might hit it – he said he didn't know which was why he didn't want the baby in the car. Great! So, off I go alone to the parking lot, only to find I'd pulled up just far enough for someone to park behind me. So much for rocking back and forth! Since there was no longer a chance of the car blowing up, I returned to the mall to get Jo Ellen and Jeri.

"What are you going to do?" Jo Ellen asked upon seeing our new state of affairs.

"Well, I'm going to find someone, somewhere that can help us," I said as I began to canvas the parking lot for our Good Samaritan. (Jo Ellen began canvassing the parking lot for a place to hide lest any of her friends show up.) There were about five men not far from us, standing around talking. I just marched myself right over to them and explained the situation. I asked if they could help me pick the car up and move it. What else could I do? It was a small Datsun (the ancestor of the Nissan). How heavy could it be? After they realized I wasn't drunk and that I was dead serious, they got behind the car and as I drove forward, they lifted the back wheels up and over the planter box. Jo Ellen and Jeri got back into the car and we drove home as if nothing had happened – unless you count Jo Ellen laughing hysterically the entire trip.

One day Jeri e-mailed me a graphic of two grocery sacks (side by side) with various grocery items protruding from the top of the sacks. The subject of the e-mail was *grocery list* but nothing was in the body of the e-mail – just the graphic. I looked at it and looked at it, thinking it was one of those puzzles like you see in the newspaper where you're supposed to circle the differences between the two pictures. Only problem was – there were no differences! I finally gave up, and called her. "Mom, I just thought you'd like to print several copies, cut them, and use them for your grocery list." Oops, again. (Hopefully it isn't in the genes, Honey, and the "ism" cycle has stopped.)

Just last summer I pulled off another "Debism" to the delight of my family who have been rolling in the floors of their homes all year while the story spread through the Barrington Clan.

It all started when Matthew and I realized that due to our schedules, I would have to take all three of our pets, lovingly referred to as *The Zoo Crew*, to the vet for their yearly shots; and he would have to meet me there to help herd them home.

So I loaded up BJ (the neurotic, diabetic cat) into his pet taxi – and this was no easy feat. It took almost 30 minutes to coax him from beneath the bed. My initial approach was food, but he must have overheard our "vet visit" conversation and he wouldn't budge. I finally resorted to dangling a shoe string in front of his little kitty eyes knowing he couldn't resist the temptation to chase it. I was able to grab him, get him into the pet taxi and get the pet taxi into the back of the SUV.

Next I carried the huge crate that our dogs sleep in downstairs and squeezed it into the back of the SUV next to the pet taxi. Then I gathered both Rascal and Angel (said dogs), put them into the crate, and off the four of us went to the vet.

Once at the vet's office I carried the pet taxi inside and signed in at the desk. When I returned to the car to put the dogs on their tandem leash the "Debism" reared its ugly head. My thought processes are so different from the rest of the world! Anyway, in my head I was afraid that while I hooked one dog to the leash the other might jump out of the car. The only logical thing to do [I thought] would be to climb into the SUV beside the crate, shut the hatch, fasten both dogs to the leash and then all three of us would get out. At the time it made so much sense to me.

My plan was working famously. I got into the back of the SUV and the door closed behind me. I got the dogs onto their leash and went to open the door. That's when I realized there was no door handle on the inside of the hatch. "Not to worry." I told myself, "I'll leave the dogs in the back, climb over the seat, go out the back door, come around, open the hatch, get the dogs out, and the world would be a beautiful place." That's when, to my utter horror, I realized the hem of my dress was caught in the hatch door.

So there I sat in the back of my SUV with no way to get out. The two dogs were on the leash, the hot Georgia sun was roasting us, Matthew was at least 20 minutes away, BJ was in his taxi wondering where the human and those dreadful canines were, and I was wondering aloud how I continually get myself into these fixes.

My brain went into overdrive trying to figure out what to do next, all the while trying to keep from panicking. I explored my options – there weren't any. As I was trying to calculate how long we could survive in the hot car, I realized my purse was jabbing me in the back and my cell phone was inside! I did the only thing I could do – I called the vet's office and explained what I'd done. Once she stopped laughing, she choked out that she'd send someone right out.

I've come to terms with "Debisms" and understand that I will most likely continue to entertain the throngs until I breathe my last. The lesson to be learned is to LAUGH – don't take life so seriously that you can't laugh during your "ism" days.

Psalm 126:2a – **Then was our mouth filled with laughter, and our tongue with singing**: (KJV)

Chapter 5
Divorced and Surviving Single

Remember how I told you I used to be pious? In 1974 the pastor at my church accepted the call from another congregation. I was a member of a Baptist church where the membership voted on who their next pastor would be. Would you believe I was one of the few (I think there was a total of three) dissenting votes because the candidate believed it was all right for a divorced person to be remarried in the church? I'm ashamed to admit I believed he shouldn't be our pastor because of that one belief.

Have you ever heard, "What goes around comes around?" It came around for me in 1990. I had married in 1974 and was sure that it was for life, but that isn't how it worked out. We married *till death do us part* but the only death in our case was the marriage itself.

Once the divorce was final I was a single mom, having never lived on my own and having never bothered to learn some of the things I really should have learned about life. That was a major drawback to my *world in a box*. The real world was a lot different from my imaginary world.

I felt all my hopes and dreams had vanished. I had to keep functioning because Jeri and James depended on me, but I was constantly trying to figure it all out and trying to determine just when and where it all went wrong.

Know what I learned? Rarely is one thing or one time or one place the problem when a marriage ends. It's usually many things, many times, and many places.

Since I come from a long line of survivors, I eventually got it together. God, family, good friends and a good therapist helped me through that difficult period in my life. As we dance through this chapter of my garage, more of my uniquely Debi methods will surface. Who knows? Maybe something will be just the thing to help someone else face similar circumstances.

There were a few projects I did on my own – not always (okay, NEVER) by the book.

One of my first projects was to replace the stereo speakers. They were making a rattling sound so I took them apart and set off to one of the electronics stores to purchase new ones. My speakers were ancient and consisted of a cabinet with a big hole where a huge wooden frame held a tiny little speaker into place in the middle. No stores sold speakers mounted into wooden frames anymore. All I could find was the speaker itself, with no way to mount it. I needed speakers so I bought two small speakers and headed home, trying to figure out how in the world I was going to attach them in the hole where the wooden frame had previously been. Just like on television, a light bulb appeared above my head – well, maybe there wasn't a light bulb, but the answer came to me.

I stopped at the hardware store to implement what I'm sure would win the best *necessity is the mother of invention award* if there were such an award. Both speakers were in small metal frames with holes on each side, so I purchased eight metal brackets containing holes. I also purchased screws to fit through the holes and nuts to hold them tight. When I got home I attached one end of a bracket where the wooden frame had been and the other end of the bracket to the metal frame around the speaker. I did this to all four sides of each speaker – and ta-da – it worked! The speakers were suspended in air by the brackets and once the front mesh covering was back in place on the front of the speaker cabinet, no one could tell what the inside looked like. I used those speakers for another six years.

I also repaired my toilet even though I had absolutely no experience with plumbing. When the flusher handle broke, I had no clue how to replace it. I fiddled around in the tank and got the broken piece out and set out to purchase one just like it. No one sold THAT particular brand (of course not) and no other brand would fit properly (of course not). Does this sound familiar? Not to be outdone, I headed back home with my broken flusher part and proceeded to open the back of the toilet again to see if I could figure out exactly how it was supposed to work. I couldn't. Then the light bulb appeared above my head again (I told you, I DO have common sense, it just sometimes takes awhile to kick in) and I realized the toilet in the other bathroom was identical. I removed the back of the other toilet to see how it was supposed to work. Once I understood how it worked, I got some heavy-duty string (yes, I used string) and tied the broken toilet piece every way imaginable so it would function in the same manner as the other toilet. It looked like a mummy toilet but it worked. My dad was amazed the string didn't break. I'll admit it was rather strange having a string cascading from the toilet tank where the handle had been, but it flushed our toilet and was a great conversation piece.

The scariest project I undertook was replacing the heating sensor in my electric dryer. I looked in the owner's manual and found the 1-800 number for trouble-shooting. Once I explained the problem, the technician told me exactly what part to get and said I could call back once I'd purchased it and someone would walk me through the installation process. I ordered the part and once it came in, I felt fine. The owner's manual had the schematic (I do know SOME technical terms) and once I had the back of the dryer off I was able to locate the part. It had three different colored wires coming out three different sides. The part didn't seem to have a top or bottom so I wasn't sure I'd remember what color went where once I took the old part off. Not to worry. I got colored markers and marked on the dryer back which color went where. In no time my dryer was fixed.

Through all my single years God sustained me, walked with me every step of the way and sent people my way that eased my burden.

Psalm 63:7 – **Because you are my help, I sing in the shadow of your wings.** (NIV)

Chapter 6
With This Ring

One day in the Summer of 1993 my grandmother told me I needed to start dating again because, as she put it, "The kids will grow up and leave one day and you don't want to be alone." So like any obedient grandchild, I set about to start dating again.

Well, let's see – how on earth does one get back into the dating scene? *The Dating Game* was no longer on the air, so that wasn't an option! Do I run a full page ad in the paper announcing that I am now interested in dating? Do I hire one of those planes to fly over pulling a sign behind it saying Debi is now back on the market?

Let's see. Plan A was my church, but it didn't even have a single's class, much less a single's group. Plan B was a single's group at another church, but all of the men who showed any interest in me were old enough to be my grandfather or, to coin a phrase, "one brick shy of a load." Plan C was a neighbor introducing me to "the perfect man for you." Mr. Perfect wasn't.

Finally, in September 1994, I met my soul mate – Matthew. It was a blind date of sorts. We have a mutual friend – okay, okay – this is the moment of truth. I'll explain exactly how Matthew and I met. It was Plan D. (Matthew's comment upon hearing that I was actually putting this in the book: "the horror!")

I was sitting home minding my own business when the telephone rang. It was nearly supper time so, of course, it was a tele-marketer. I usually don't talk with them but for some reason (must have been a weak moment or perhaps destiny) I decided to hear this one out. The purpose of her call was to interest me in making an appointment at a dating service. Yes, it was definitely a weak moment, because I made the appointment.

The big day came and I was terrified. I went in for my appointment and ended up joining (I told you it was a weak moment). I chose the least expensive plan, which was the *Picture Book* plan. They took my picture and I filled out a form listing my likes/dislikes/interests/etc. Each page contained a photo of the person with a copy of the form he/she had filled in with his/her likes/dislikes/interests/etc. The object was to look through several books and make a list of the ones you were interested in meeting. Once you turned in the list, they would mail your information sheet (without your picture) to each person(s) you had selected, along with a note encouraging him to give you a call. No last names were used so I felt it was fairly safe, although I must admit that I was still a nervous wreck.

Anyway, I made my selections and waited for the phone to start ringing. I think I received about three or four calls, including Matthew, but he's the only one I decided to meet. I was very impressed with him on the phone and actually canceled a meeting with one of the other men who had called before Matthew.

We discovered that he worked with a friend of mine from church which made me much more comfortable with the situation because I didn't feel he was a total stranger anymore. As soon as Matthew and I hung up, I called my friend to get the scoop on Matthew. I found out later that Matthew had sought him out the next day at work to get the scoop on me.

Several months later we were discussing what we had told our parents regarding how we met. Without even planning to do so, we had both told virtually the same story – "we have a mutual friend." Well, it wasn't a fib. We did have a mutual friend, and we never said that he introduced us. It's funny looking back because we were both grown and should have been able to just tell them we'd met through a dating service. Oh well, guess they know now...

Even though we had both been hurt in our previous marriages, we knew we had to take the risk to love each other. We were never at a lack for words. Most of our religious and political views were similar, and the ones that were different seemed to compliment one another and cause us to really THINK DEEPLY and, thereby, grow. One of my friends called us two peas in a pod. That's exactly how we felt.

I'm not sure when Matthew figured out that he loved me, but I knew he was a keeper after the second date and I knew for sure that I was in love with him sitting in the rain at a *Grass Roots* concert in Roswell, GA, in August 1995.

On December 22, 1995, Matthew proposed – and I accepted. Upon hearing that Matthew and I were getting married, my sister Gail said, "You do realize that you're marrying Poppy, right?" [My sisters call Dad, Poppy.] I hadn't thought much about that, but it turns out that she was right (I hate it when that happens).

Matthew and Dad are both "Mr. Clean" – which is a good thing, because they help around the house. I didn't realize until recently though, just how **much** they are alike. When Matthew dusts, he uses the vacuum cleaner (that little round brush that I always thought was just a cute extra piece). I was talking to Mom the other day and heard the vacuum in the background. She explained it was new and that Daddy was just having the best time playing with his new toy. I made the offhand comment, "Well at least he isn't vacuuming the pictures on the wall."

There was dead silence on the other end. Then slowly Mom replied, "Uh, that's exactly what he's doing." Good grief, I HAVE married my Daddy!

Matthew and I wanted our three children to have a part in the wedding ceremony so Jeri sang, James gave me away, and Jena held the rings. The only guests were both sets of parents and the pastor's wife. We videotaped the service and, wouldn't you know it, the audio part did not work. We actually had the pastor come to our house a few weeks later to recreate the service on a cassette tape so we could play it while the video tape was playing on the screen. When we tried to play the two at the same time, the words and our mouths never quite jived, making it look like a Japanese film with English voice-overs. Of course, the video tape mishap was just the first of many in our life together...the "Debisms" appear to be contagious.

I'd be lying if I said we never disagree. Of course we do; however, the neat thing about our relationship is that we talk it out – sometimes more loudly than other times. We work at our relationship and sometimes it takes a lot of work. Marriage is like wine. It gets better with age if you handle the relationship carefully the way a wine maker handles the grapes. We're honest with one another and we love each other enough to know our disagreements don't diminish that love. We respect the other's opinions, and though we will never agree on some topics, we accept each other – warts and all. We grow in our ability to understand that it is OK to disagree. The key is agreeing to disagree while always respecting the other's point of view. We learn from each other and, while it may not change our opinion, we accept that **1 + 1 = 2** is the same answer as

$$\begin{array}{r} 1 \\ +1 \\ \hline 2 \end{array}$$

Neither answer is incorrect, the method is just different.

What happens when we reach an impasse? For us it's like a jump ball in basketball – one team gets the ball and the other doesn't, but the game continues. It's give and take just like in any other area of life. Life with Matthew is truly an adventure – one I wouldn't miss for the world. That whole Venus/Mars thing is lost on us, because we're both from Pluto. And now there's the question of whether Pluto is even a planet. Great!

I understand major problems arise in marriages and sometimes staying married isn't an option. I understand because I've been there. I also understand that my first husband and I didn't realize that marriage was work and we didn't protect, honor, appreciate, and care for our relationship. My hope in sharing my story is that people who need to know will understand that when a husband and wife love **and** respect each other, their differences won't destroy them, but will make them stronger. This is the epitome of true companionship.

Genesis 2:24 – **For this reason a man will leave his father and his mother and be united to his wife, and they will become one flesh.** (NIV)

PART TWO

Relationships
It's All Relative...Usually

You met me in Part One. You also met two of the important men in my life, Daddy and Matthew. Now it's time to meet some more people in my life – mostly family, with an occasional good friend sprinkled in for good measure. Each one has made contributions that have helped me become who I am. Most of the contributions have been positive; but, some have been negative. Even negative, bad experiences have value because they require us to reach deep down inside ourselves to overcome them.

Chapter 1
Beck's Bad Girl

My maternal grandmother's name was Rebecca Hogg Steppe. I called her Mommy Steppe, but most of her friends called her Beck. Mother was her 3rd (and youngest) child and always talked about writing an autobiography entitled *Beck's Bad Girl*. What better title for a chapter about my mother?

As long as I can remember, her name was *Mother* because she made it very clear to me at a very early age that *Mom, Mama, Mum*, etc., were not acceptable to her. I remember thinking as a teenager that my kids could call me anything but MOTHER, which is too formal for my tastes.

On the surface, and to the outside world, our relationship appeared normal. However, Mother and I had an extremely complex relationship. The purpose of this chapter is to share some of our experiences, both good and bad, in the hopes that someone in a similar relationship with a parent may benefit.

There wasn't much physical abuse, just an occasional slap across the face, an occasional push against the wall, an occasional yank on my hair, or an occasional pinching. Mother's arsenal was mostly verbal and emotional. She could spew the words with more venom than any snake you've ever encountered.

I don't remember bad times as a young child, but sometime after Mommy Steppe's death in 1962 and

Mother's cancer diagnosis in 1963, life with Mother changed drastically. She was never the same after those two events. She shut most of her friends out of her life during those two years, and in 1964 when we moved to Charleston, she shut the rest of them out. It was as if she died – even though she was still breathing. There weren't many help-groups in those days (at least none that we knew of) but I doubt she would have taken advantage of the opportunity even if there had been one because she had a stigma about receiving assistance for mental and/or emotional problems. She considered people who sought that type of help to be crazy.

As I write this, it occurs to me that she suffered three major, life-changing, stress-causing events in three years. Her mother died (1962), she was diagnosed with breast cancer (1963), and she had to move from the city where she had grown up (1964). No wonder she was depressed. And since she didn't get professional help, no wonder she was unable to cope.

Mother was a Sunday School teacher and was in church every time the doors were opened. She wore a facade in public but Daddy and I knew the woman behind the mask. Her life at church and her life at home were very different. People we knew rarely caught any glimpse of what happened within the walls of our home. Occasionally she would be unable to control her anger in public, but people who witnessed that saw only the tip of an anger iceberg that submerged itself deep beneath the surface of my mother's personality.

She held everyone else to such a high standard of Christian ethics and yet I can remember being backed against a wall with her face just inches from mine as she spewed venom at me, all the while wearing her monster face. Her monster face was the face of a crazed person. It was classic Hollywood at its best. Picture all the wild, truly crazy characters that you've ever seen in any thriller and you'll be staring right at Mother's monster face. Even writing about it now gives me chill bumps and transports me back many decades.

Most of these episodes would end with Mother sitting in her chair and me sitting on the floor at her feet begging her forgiveness. The word *groveling* comes to mind as I replay those tapes in my head. These sessions usually lasted most of the night and into the wee hours of the morning. And the odd thing is, Mother would call in sick and not go to work, while I was expected to go to school or work (once I graduated high school). I can't explain why I didn't leave home once I became an adult.

I'm living proof that abuse without bruises is still abuse and debating what is worse – bruises or no bruises – is like debating which came first, the chicken or the egg. It is a ridiculous argument because both types of abuse are equally bad for the people living through them. It's how we react to the situation and what we do with our lives once we get out of the abusive situation that sets the tone for how we live the rest of our life.

I never let Mother meet me. She only knew the little girl she tried so hard to create. I've often wondered what her reaction would have been to meeting the real me, the one who was buried deep inside all the years. Someone once commented to me that my mother was rolling in her grave at something I'd just done. My comeback: "She's in a constant spin cycle!"

I think her faith evolved into something far removed from what it started out to be. It was like she felt that only she knew what was best and only her ideas were the right ones. In all of Mother's madness, I'm sure she loved God the only way she knew how and I'm just as sure that she is with Him today. She died in the early morning hours of September 18, 1973.

Her battle with cancer had lasted ten years and during those ten years I had prayed every night that she would be cured. When the doctor told us that she had less than a week to live, I reeled from the news. How can this be? Where is GOD? That night I grabbed the Bible, daring God to speak to me. What happened next is nothing short of a miracle to me because I was angry with God for not answering my prayer and I really had no clue what I was looking for in the Scripture. The Bible fell open to Psalm 46. Verse 1 reads: **God is our refuge and strength, a very present help in trouble.** Verse 10a reads: **Be still and know that I am God.** And then, as I turned the pages randomly, the Bible fell open to Psalm 120:1 – **In my distress I cried unto the Lord, and He heard me.** And also on that page Psalm 121:1 – **I will lift up mine eyes unto the hills, from whence cometh my help.** (KJV)

Once Mother died, my anger toward her began to take root and live inside me for many years. It led me to make poor choices. Once my children were born, I found myself becoming my mother. I'll never forget the night that I pulled Jeri's hair just because she didn't understand her homework assignment. She was in kindergarten at the time and wore her hair in pigtails. I actually grabbed each one and pulled in opposite directions. I'm weeping as I write this because it's as vivid now as the night 24 years ago when it happened. I remember feeling shocked and ashamed that I'd done that. That night was a turning point in my life.

As a result of my anger I began counseling, trying to make sense of some of the things in my life. Through counseling I came to understand my mother better and to realize that the love I had for her was real. She was my mother and I DID LOVE HER in spite of everything that happened. I also realized that I was in a *history repeating itself* mode, but that it wasn't too late to change courses. I came to realize that Mother had suffered abuse at the hands of her mother. I made the decision that the cycle of abuse would end with Mother – I would not continue to abuse my children.

I learned from people who had known her for years, that she'd always been a *my way or the highway* type of person and that she would rarely, if ever, bend. I can only guess that the reason I don't remember the abuse as a young child is because I didn't buck her system. But as I got older and began to challenge her she felt threatened and felt she had to tighten the reigns.

I'm not sure of her reasons or even if they were conscious, but she did abuse me. And yet when I visited her grave in April 1988 and told her all the things I was afraid to say while she was alive and all the feelings that had built up inside me since her death, I heard her speak to me. She said, "I'm sorry. I loved you and I did the best I could." I heard her speak, I felt her presence and I forgave her on that day.

Mother's last years were difficult to experience but, as with many bad experiences, I learned some valuable lessons:

I have learned that as long as I'm in my right mind and can control my thoughts and actions, I will live until there is no breath left in my body.

I have learned that circumstances don't dictate the life you will have – your reaction to the circumstances dictates the life you will have.

I have learned to accept my children for who they are and I've learned to allow them their own identity, even when their choices differ from the choices I would make for them.

I have learned that even though I wasn't a perfect mother, I did the best I could at the time and, in retrospect, so did my mother. The major difference is that I got professional help when I realized I needed it.

I have learned that I am a survivor and I get that quality from my mother. She overcame much in life prior to marrying Daddy and becoming my mother – her brother died when hot tar was spilt on him as he was roofing a building in Macon; she watched as her first husband and niece drowned during a boating accident in Florida; she watched her sister die an agonizing death from spinal cancer. She survived each tragedy because she held onto the hand of God – and she taught me to do the same.

I have learned to never give up hope.

I have learned that I can hold a grudge, be unhappy, sad, bitter, and blame all my problems on Mother, or I can forgive her and move on with my life. I've chosen the latter and I've forgiven *Beck's Bad Girl*. She did, after all, bring me into this world and without her influence in my life I would not be who I am today.

Chapter 2
Not By Blood

When Dad and Margie announced to us that they were getting married, I asked if she minded if I called her *Mom* since I called my mother *Mother*. With tears in her eyes, she responded she would be honored.

I've known Mom my whole life. She and Mother were very good friends, so she was always a part of my life. For many years her family and ours attended the same church and our lives were intertwined. She has always been there for the important events in my life long before she officially became my Mom. When Mommy Steppe died, Mother went down like the *Titanic* and Mom rushed to my rescue. She took care of me during the funeral and the days following when Mother wasn't able to do so.

I stayed with Mom's family during the two weeks Mother was in the hospital following her mastectomy. She gently explained to me what breast cancer was and all about Mother's surgery using words that a ten-year-old would understand.

She was there for me as I planned my first wedding the year after Mother died. Having grown up a tomboy, I was at a total loss when it came to planning a wedding and all of the things that go along with it. Mom was there for me every step of the way and was the mother of the bride in every sense of the phrase. Even when the big day came and I realized the department store hadn't made the necessary alterations to my wedding dress!

Who knew I was supposed to actually take it out of the bag and try it on when I picked it up to insure everything was fine after the alterations? Well, Mom knew and she asked me if I had. I told her that I hadn't thought of it but I was sure everything would be fine. I had already taken the dress to my friend's house by that time and never even thought about Mom's suggestion again. When I went to pick up the dress the morning of my wedding, I realized the pins were still in it and no alterations had been done at all! Mom never said the dreaded, "I told you so." Instead, she called the store where I'd purchased the dress and explained the situation to them. As I was driving up the driveway to our house, Dad was backing down it and I literally handed the dress to him through the window so that he could take it back to the mall.

The wedding was at 2:00 p.m. and Dad returned with my altered wedding gown a little after 1:00. Mom had done her best to keep me calm by styling my hair and helping me with all the preliminaries so that all I had to do was slip into the dress. Slip into the dress I did and then we made the mad dash to the church which was thankfully only five minutes away.

Mom has a way with words. Recently, I was telling her of a problem we were having with our air conditioner – on one of the hottest days of the year so far. I was hot and frustrated, but Mom's words brought a smile to my face and melted my frustration away when she commented, "It just takes the syrup right out of you, doesn't it?"

Mom is continually sending just the right card with just the right verse to fit whatever it is I'm experiencing at the time. It's so wonderful to receive those cards. I'm convinced she has the Spiritual gift of healing – healing of the weary, healing of the down-trodden, healing of anyone who is suffering through whatever it may be. A card from my mom is healing balm for any situation.

Even when her own mother passed away, Mom said the most beautiful words to me: "You are the only one of my daughters who knows what I'm going through now." What a beautiful gift to give me on one of the worst days of her life!

We don't always agree – and like most mothers and daughters we've had our moments, but when those times occur we've both learned to speak our peace and then move on with our relationship still in tact. That's the way any mother and daughter should relate and react to one another.

Mom is the only maternal grandmother my children know and she loves them just as she does her biological grandchildren. And she is just beside herself with Mackenzie and Macyn, the great-grands!

Mom is a wonderful lady and I've learned so much about life, about mothering, and about grand-mothering from her. No, we're not related by blood, but I love her as if I were her flesh and blood and as far as I'm concerned, she is my mother. She has built our family upon the foundation of love. Her faith in Christ and her love for Him shows in all she does.

Proverbs 31:30 – **Charm is deceptive, and beauty is fleeting; but a woman who fears the Lord is to be praised.** (NIV)

Chapter 3
My Tribute

When my phone rang in the wee hours of the morning the Saturday before Father's Day in 2004, I knew before I answered that something was wrong. My Aunt Lois was calling from Pensacola, FL, to tell me that Granny had fallen, was in the hospital and not expected to live. She called me because she felt Dad should hear the news in person instead of over the phone.

I tried to digest what I'd just heard. Jeri, Wes, Mackenzie, Matthew, and I were planning to join my parents for a July 4th trip to Pensacola in order to introduce Mackenzie to the rest of her family. We had the "five generation" picture all planned. It was only three weeks away. Granny had been so excited to hear about the birth of her latest great-great-grand! She was looking forward to our trip, and now she was dying!

I pulled myself together enough to call Kathy, my oldest sister, to seek her advice on how to tell Dad. It was agreed that he should be told in person, not over the phone. The plan was for me to drive to our parents' home and for her to meet me there.

I quickly packed for the trip to Pensacola and drove to their house. It was almost 6:00 a.m. when Kathy and I drove up within minutes of each other. One of the saddest things I have ever heard was Dad's end of the conversation he had with Lois that morning. The last words he said before they hung up were, "Tell Mother to hold on – I'm on the way."

My parents and I were on the road for Pensacola (a six-hour trip) before 8:00 that morning. Granny wasn't able to hold on and died before we arrived.

Lois asked two of my cousins and me to say a few words at Granny's funeral. I remember waking up in the middle of the night and writing my thoughts on a paper napkin because I didn't know where any paper was. I'm not sure how or why the plans changed, but none of the grandchildren had the opportunity to speak at her funeral. Here's what I would have said:

"We are here today to honor one of the finest ladies I have ever known, Janie Knight Barrington – Granny.

She taught us everything we need to know – we didn't have to learn it in kindergarten – we learned it at the feet of our grandmother.

Examples of what she taught us:
1) Be a Christian not only on Sunday, but every day of every week of every year.
2) Never judge others.
3) Never utter harsh or unkind words.
4) Take life in stride.
5) Don't *put on airs* – she was the most real person I knew.

She loved having her house filled with Barringtons, in spite of our somewhat dysfunctional tendencies.

She was the perfect example of a grandmother:
1) She gave the best back rubs in the world – many times two grandkids at a time.
2) She taught me the love of putting jigsaw puzzles together.

3) She tried to teach me to cook – somehow that gene skipped me – but she still tried.
4) She laughed often and her eyes danced when she smiled.
5) She gave awesome hugs.

She was my first example of how to be a stepmother and because of her example I knew the fairy tales had it all wrong. She married my widowed grandfather who had seven children – the youngest was my Dad. She and my grandfather had four children. Most of her grandchildren were *steps*. I never witnessed any partiality. She loved us all and she was proud of us all.

I remember calling her many times and saying "Hey, Granny," and she'd say, "Hey, Debi."

Then I'd say, "How do you always know it's me?"

"Because you're my granddaughter," was always her response.

Later in life my Dad became a stepfather and we became a blended family. No problem, because Granny had already taught him what he needed to know.

In 1996 I became a stepmother and my children became part of a blended family – no problem, because Granny had already taught me what I needed to know.

She taught without preaching.

She taught without railing.

She taught without judging.

Today we honor her life because she taught us all how to live".

Proverbs 31:10 – **Who can find a virtuous woman? For her price is far above rubies. (KJV)**

Chapter 4
Siblings – Just Because I Wasn't One Doesn't Mean I'm Not One

In some ways I can't relate to the sibling relationship because when Dad and Mom married I was an adult and became a sibling overnight. The fact that Mom was a family friend whose children I had grown up with has, however, given me a history with my three sisters. Even though it wasn't exactly a sibling history, it did mirror sibling relationships to some extent.

Kathy is two and half years older than I, Gail is one and half years younger than I, and Jo Ellen is seven and half years younger than I. Kathy and Gail were my playmates when I lived in Macon and Jo Ellen was the pain in the behind that tagged along after us older kids – sounds like siblings to me!

Gail was always a little lady – we called her *Miss Hollywood* – but Kathy and I were both tomboys. Kathy and I did all kinds of things that I'd have had a cardiac if my kids had done. I don't think there was anything that we wouldn't try in those days. If Kathy tried something, I'd try it, too – sounds like siblings to me!

Once Kathy and I wanted to see how it felt to be black so we covered our faces, arms, and legs with charcoal. You should have seen the bath water that night.

Then, there was the time that Gail and I were playing dress-up at my house. I'm not sure where Kathy was, but it was just the two of us – until Jo Ellen toddled into the room. Now about a week before that, Jo Ellen had somehow gotten under their house and eaten some cotton dust and had to have her stomach pumped out. So when she toddled in and began to DRINK the liquid makeup Mother had given me to play with, Gail and I didn't know what to do. Given what had just happened to Jo Ellen, the eight and nine year olds had a decision to make. Did we just wait and see if she got sick or did we tell? What's worse, her getting sick or our getting in trouble for not paying close enough attention to her? Tell me that isn't a sibling thought process. [By the way, Jo Ellen was fine and to my knowledge, no animals were injured in the taste test.]

One of the first things we did on the day we became siblings was to sneak a wedding cake into the house without our parents seeing it. Kathy ran interference while Gail and I hid the cake on the shelf in my bedroom closet. So far, so good; however, we forgot to take the cake when we left for the church.

The ceremony was very small and included all of us – Jo Ellen served as Mom's Maid of Honor and I played the piano for Kathy and Gail to sing. After the service, just the immediate family went to a local restaurant for dinner. It was during the meal we realized we'd left the cake at home. No problem. I called my friend Shirley who had a key to the house and asked her to bring the cake to us. Only by the grace of God did she find the cake because it never occurred to me to tell her it was on the closet shelf in my bedroom. She looked all over for that cake, and said she was sitting on the floor of my bedroom at her wit's end trying to think where we would have hidden the cake when, for no reason, she glanced up and the cake caught her eye from the closet shelf. Tell me God and Jesus weren't up in Heaven rolling on the floor with laughter after that one.

I enjoy being one of four. I enjoy being introduced as, "My sister, Debi." Or even, "My sister, Debi, the black sheep." Well, SOMEBODY'S got to be the black sheep, and it may as well be me.

Actually, that's exactly the way Gail introduced me to one of her co-workers who responded, "Why Gail, I thought YOU were the black sheep," to which Gail quickly replied, "Oh no, I'm just the **brown** sheep."

I've recently become more domesticated due to two things in my life – Weight Watchers and Stampin' Up. I figured if I was going to be a member of Weight Watchers, I ought to buy their cookbooks and actually learn how to cook. Jeri kept saying, "Mom, if you can read, you can cook." I bought the cookbooks and much to my amazement discovered she was right.

Prior to that, I'd always take something I could buy pre-made to family gatherings rather than actually try to cook something. A couple of years ago, I got brave and took my first Weight Watcher recipe to Mom's for one of our gatherings. I was so proud of myself. I made one of those layered salads and it looked just like the picture. I bought a bowl just like the one in the picture and took the cookbook down to Mom's to show everyone. [Gail had done that once with a Southern Living recipe so I knew I was supposed to take the picture.] As everyone arrived, the first thing asked was, "Who made the salad?"

"Debi," Mom would reply.

"Yeah, right – who made the salad?" I'm not sure what amazed them most – the fact that I'd made the salad or that I knew what cilantro was!

My friend, Cara McArthur (I call her *Carrots*) is also my Stampin' Up demonstrator. For the past several years, I've participated in a group that meets monthly to make greeting cards and scrapbook pages using Stampin' Up products. I also have an annual party at my house and a portion of my home office is devoted to all my stamps and accessories. After attending one of my parties and seeing all the things I'd made, Jo Ellen looked at Cara and said, "You've turned Debi into a girl!" Sounds like a sibling comment to me.

We sisters have a tradition – we go shopping together on the day after Thanksgiving. IT IS SO MUCH FUN! [Author's Note: Matthew thinks we're crazy.] We all sit around on the floor at Mom's after lunch on Thanksgiving Day and go through all the sales flyers from the newspaper, making our lists and checking them twice. We usually begin shopping round 8:00 in the morning and don't return until about 7:00 in the evening...although I must be honest and say we used to leave before 6:00 a.m. and not return until after 8:00 p.m. – but that was before three of us reached fifty.

I may not have always been a sister, but I sure am one now and it is one of the greatest experiences of my life. I am truly blessed.

Chapter 5
All My Children

I was two months shy of my 25th birthday when Jeri was born, and totally oblivious as to what I was supposed to do with this tiny little creature. Mother had never let me baby-sit and since I was an only child until I was 21, I had absolutely NO EXPERIENCE with babies. I was afraid to even try and dress Jeri before leaving the hospital so I asked the nurse to do it. Can you believe that? Even as I write this it is hard to believe that I was so unsure of myself back then, but I was. To coin an older commercial's phrase, "I've come a long way, baby."

The joy of parenthood is something I'm finding hard to put into words. The love I felt as I first looked at both Jeri and James was overwhelming. It was an all-consuming love, an unconditional love, a total and complete love.

Back in those days new mothers and their babies actually got to stay in the hospital for three days, instead of the revolving-door approach used now. Those three days are very necessary in my opinion, because it gives the new mom some down time to rest and recover before going home to her new reality. The first few weeks consist of one new experience after another, each happening so quickly it's hard to keep up even when you've had three days of rest. I can't imagine doing it with no rest.

In reality, I had no idea what to do with Jeri. Mom came over and showed me how to bathe her. I was so afraid I'd drown her or that I'd get so much soap on her she'd slip right through my hands like a bar of soap.

Other realities are the dirty diapers, the crying at all hours of the night, colic, spitting up food – the list goes on and on and on. But that's just one list – the other list goes on and on as well. Each day is a new experience. Watching them find their toes and hands is unbelievably fun and rewarding. Seeing the first tooth come in, hearing the first words, watching them crawl for the first time, and then watching that first step are all simply overwhelming.

The first days pass quickly, and then weeks and months go by and before you know it all that adds up to years, and the kids are no longer babies.

I really enjoyed the little league years, too. Running from ball field to ball field was actually fun to me. I even enjoyed the many hours spent working my turn in the concession stand. There were nights when Jeri would be playing on one field and James would be on another in the same ballpark. I would literally run through the woods between the fields so that I could see some of both games, praying all along that I'd be in the stands when one of them was up to bat or making the big play in the field.

There were many times over the years that James entertained us with his innocence. Once we were at the fair waiting in line to get our tickets. My husband asked how much the tickets were – I replied that adults were $2.00, Jeri was $1.00, and that James was free (because he was under five). He jerked my hand and retorted, "I am not *free*, I'm four." Another time on a long road trip James asked where we were. I replied that we were in the middle of nowhere. He waited about 15 minutes then asked in all seriousness, "Are we out of the middle of nowhere yet?"

Sometimes the kids and I would camp out in the living room on Friday or Saturday nights. Yes, we put up a tent and everything. It was so much fun. I felt like a kid again myself on those nights. Sometimes we'd face the opening of the tent toward the television, have popcorn and watch movies. Other times we'd sit inside the tent and play games. It was great.

The teenage years came so quickly that I was caught by surprise. All of a sudden the kids had friends to hang out with and the weekend camp-outs ended much too soon for me. (Now I've started that tradition with Mackenzie. The tent is long gone but we sleep on a blow-up mattress. Maybe I'll ask for a tent for Mother's Day...)

James took one of his first independent moves long before he became a teenager. It was the morning of his sixth birthday. I went in to wake him up, and before saying good morning or anything, he announced to me that his name was *James* not Jamie (as we had always called him) and, "Don't you think I'm a little old for Winnie the Pooh curtains?" I was stunned! He'd never even hinted that there was a problem with his name or his curtains – and all of a sudden he woke up one morning and that was it. Well, from that day forward he became James and that very day we went and bought curtains with mallard ducks (which I figured was very masculine and unlike sport's teams, etc., something he wouldn't out grow).

By the way, do you know how to purchase a $35.00 gallon of milk? You take your 17 year old son to the grocery store with you – I speak from experience. This actually happened. One day I asked James if he wanted to go to the store with me to pick up a gallon of milk. The next thing I knew, we were rolling $35.00 worth of groceries to the car.

James is 26 now and has become such a wonderful young man. I'm so proud of him and the accomplishments he's made. He has taught me to think outside the box – because he thinks outside the box. He always seems to have a slightly different twist on life and it's an education to listen to his thought processes. He makes me stretch. He makes me grow.

Jena was ten when Matthew and I married so I didn't have the opportunity to experience the early years with her. I think we've made up for lost time though, and we've built a very strong relationship with each other. We enjoy discussing our various political views – just like Dad and I used to do twenty (okay, okay THIRTY – all right, all right THIRTY-FIVE) years ago. We both enjoy playing card games and board games and spend hours trying to figure out new strategies to win. We have deep discussions into the night, and she, too, makes me think in order to argue my point. She is 22 now and doing very well. When she graduated from Oxford College of Emory University, she allowed me to do something that I'd never done before – I got to spend graduation night in her dorm room. Now, that may not sound like fun to you, but to me it was great. I'd never, ever slept in a dorm room. I was like a kid at Christmas. We ordered pizza at midnight and everything.

A strange phenomenon occurs at the age of 18. I call it the *I can do it myself/Mom HELP me* syndrome. Jeri and I actually had that conversation. One night when I was explaining to her how to handle a certain situation, she announced, "I'm 18 and can do it myself." The very next night she came to me and asked me to do something for her because "I'm only 18 and can't do it myself." I can't even put into words what was going through my head at that moment. I just remember looking her straight in the eyes with a totally confused look on my face and exclaiming, "You're CONFUSING ME!" I reminded her of the night before. She had a very sheepish look and mumbled something about needing help when she asked for it but not wanting unsolicited advice. We both had a good laugh and decided neither of us had experience in this new chapter in our lives and we'd use each other as guinea pigs.

I will never forget the time Jeri asked me what it was like to grow up in a black and white world in the olden days. At first I had no clue what on earth she meant, but quickly realized that she had been watching old T.V. shows on the cable network and all of them were in black and white. She thought the entire world was that way when I was a kid!

She has always kept me on my toes with her word usage and interpretation of said words. Two occurrences are forever etched in my brain. When Jeri was about four we purchased a child's dictionary – okay, *I* purchased the dictionary – from a door to door salesman. One day she and I were going over the various words and when we came to the word "brave" I said, "Jeri do you know what brave is?"

She put her little hands on her hips, looked at me like I had lost my mind and said, "Everyone knows they're a baseball team!"

The other time was when she was five and had said something unkind to James. To this day I don't know what she said, but I know it wasn't good. I asked her what she'd said and she replied, "Nothing."

I really wanted to know what she said so I kept pressing, using all of my parenting skills (I didn't have many). Finally, I said, "Well God knows what you said." She didn't miss a beat. Her reply, as only a five-year-old wise guy could say: "Then ask Him what I said!" ARGH!!!!!!!!

In addition to being my daughter, Jeri is also one of my best friends. She and I enjoy many of the same things: reading, writing, jokes (I think she inherited my off-the-wall sense of humor), e-mails, sentimental things that make us cry, going for long walks, going to plays – just to name a few. Even during the tumultuous teenage years, she and I remained close. She always confided in me and I was so thankful for that. There were many times when she'd have a sleep over and she and her friends would invite me to watch the scary movies with them because they enjoyed watching me hide my eyes. (Okay, okay – I'm 54 and still can't watch scary movies.)

One of my most cherished presents from Jeri is a book about mothers and daughters, celebrating the closeness and the relationship that we have. It is filled with memories and pictures that tell our story. Jeri is 29 and it seems just yesterday a nurse was dressing her so that I could bring her home…

Kids are ours for a short period of time. We have only so long to mold them into the adults that they will become. Make the most of the opportunity you have to build strong relationships with your children.

Psalm 127:3 – **Lo, children *are* an heritage of the Lord: *and* the fruit of the womb is *his* reward.** (KJV)

Chapter 6
Happy Holidays!

WOW – there are people everywhere! This is HUGE! It's the family I always dreamed of having – and I don't have to wash CLEAN dishes to get it! (See Part 1, Chapter 1 – in case you've forgotten.)

That's how I felt the first Thanksgiving after Mom and Dad married. We were celebrating Thanksgiving in Georgia at *AuntieMa* and *UncPa's* house and there were 13 in attendance that day. Perhaps some clarification is due at this point. Mom's sister (Kitty) and brother-in-law (Tommy) are *AuntieMa* and *UncPa*. When our children began to be born we gave Kitty and Tommy the names *AuntieMa* and *UncPa*. It made perfect sense to us.

That holiday was the first of many that I have enjoyed since Mom, my sisters, and *AuntieMa* became a part of my family. Now, due to all the marriages and births, there are even more of us. Kathy is married to Tink (don't ask) and their daughters are Amy (married to Curt) and Julie (married to Jason); Gail's son is Mark (married to Mary); Jo Ellen is married to Brad and their son is Joel and their daughter is Kaylin. Kitty and Tommy's son David is married to Roxanne, and they have two daughters, Rachel and Melissa. We have grown to a total of 28. [We buried UncPa as this book was being completed.]

My parents moved from Charleston to the Atlanta area in the late 1980's, so now most of our family gatherings are at their house. The entire clan gathers for Thanksgiving, Christmas, and Easter; and then most of us show up for various birthdays and any other excuse we can make up to be together and eat. Since some of the grandchildren are married now we are having to share with in-laws, but we're trying to adjust – sometimes we make a *to go* box for them; other times we just eat their portion and pretend they were there.

Talk about family traditions –our family should win a prize. We have two traditions that are unique.

First of all, Mom has a rule that all grandchildren (Mark, Jeri, Amy, James, Julie, Jena, Joel, and Kaylin) MUST hunt eggs on Easter Sunday – that is, until they marry. I really think the rule went into effect when Mark (the oldest) hit his teens and began to question having to hunt the eggs with the little ones. But what goes around comes around, because when Mark was 25, James was 16 and starting asking the same question. Mark grabbed him (in the nicest way possible of course) and said something to the effect, "I'm 25 years old and still hunt eggs, get your basket and get out there and find those eggs."

Four grandchildren have now reached non-egg-hunting status due to marriage: Mark and Jeri last hunted in 2000 – he was 28 and she was 22; Amy last hunted in 2003 – she was 24; Julie last hunted in 2007 – she was 24. James at age 26 was the oldest hunter in 2007. Julie was 2nd, Jena was 3rd at age 21, Joel was 4th at age 19, and Kaylin rounded out the pack of grandkids at age 9. However, now that we have Mackenzie and Macyn (the great-grands) I'm sure the hunts will continue.

Another family tradition is that each grandchild, great-grandchild, and grand-niece has to work for his or her Christmas presents in ways only Mom can dream up. She gathers all of them around her on the floor of her living room and then the fun begins. One year she actually bought TWO each of several different little golden books so that she could cut the pictures out and glue them back into the matching book, hiding money behind said pictures. You should have seen all of them rubbing each of the pages trying to find the pictures with the hidden money. Another year she created her own version of a scavenger hunt, and they each had to follows clues to their individual gift. And yet another year she taped money into individual match boxes and then taped each match box shut with about four rolls of invisible tape. It was a race to finish that year, and only a few nails were broken.

Strange but true, our wonderfully dysfunctional family spends our holidays this way and I wouldn't have it any other way. Mom is creating wonderful memories for the kids as well as us adults – even though once or twice I've heard someone say, "Grandmama, you've got WAY to much time on your hands." It's great being part of the Barrington clan – great indeed!

Oddly enough, the *Barrington Family* is not mentioned in the Scripture; however, I did find a verse that captures the essence of why families are blessed. It was God's promise to Abraham. Genesis 12:3b **and in thee shall all families of the earth be blessed. (KJV)**

Chapter 7
The Grand Entrances!

Mackenzie

TA-DA! Everyone wants an entrance that will be memorable. We want people to look up and take notice when we enter. Mackenzie Mara Brown is no different from anyone else.

All she wanted was a little attention and WOW did she make us all sit up and take notice. She had us all on the edge of our seats. She had us pacing back and forth, up and down, all around the hallways. But before I jump right into my story, let me back up and give you a little bit of history on Miss Mackenzie Brown.

My little girl, Jeri, grew up and met her Prince Charming, Wes. They got married and were living happily ever after until one day they decided that something, or someone, was missing from their family and they decided to have a baby. Once Jeri got pregnant, they dreamt up various and unique ways of telling each of the family members – all three sets of grandparents-to-be, as well as one set of great-grandparents-to-be, and two great-grandmothers-to-be. No announcement was the same.

We invited Jeri and Wes over for supper one night in May of 2003. As we were beginning our meal, Jeri asked if we wanted to see a new outfit that she had gotten that day. "Sure," we replied, and out of her bag she produced a baby sleeper. I sat there blinking and trying to get my mind to compute why on earth Jeri would buy a baby sleeper (it was a true "Debism" if ever there was one). All of a sudden the little man that runs around through the circuits of my brain helping me process thoughts got to wherever he needed to be for my light bulb moment and I realized, *"I'm going to be a GRANDMOTHER!"* I was so happy and rendered totally speechless for a moment (that doesn't happen often).

And so began the journey to the grand entrance, which Jeri told us was scheduled for January 30, 2004. Now since my birthday is February 7th and since most first babies don't come on schedule, I commented that if the baby was a week late, we would share a birthday. Jeri gave me *the look* and said that wasn't happening.

Jeri chronicled her progress week by week and sent e-mails to all of her family and close friends. We read with amazement and awe the various changes going on inside her. The baby was developing into a little person we were all very excited to meet. We all oohed and aahed over the sonogram pictures that she e-mailed us. They even had a DVD made and brought it to the house for us to ooh and aah some more.

Thanks to modern technology, handheld heart monitors are now available for a small fortune, uh, I mean fee, to listen to your baby's heartbeat in the comfort of your own home. I'll never forget the day Jeri called because she had a surprise for me at her office and wanted me to drop by on my way home from work. When I arrived, she closed the door and I was awe struck as I heard my grandchild's heartbeat for the very first time. What an amazing experience that was!

As the date of arrival approached, we all became more and more excited. And then the big day came....and went...with no baby. I never gave up on the idea that Baby Brown (the one thing Jeri didn't share was a name) might be born on my birthday. Jeri, however, had other plans and the doctor induced labor on February 5th. Baby Brown, as it turned out, had plans of her own, and really wanted to *hang in there* so to speak.

I lost count of the family members and friends that came and went during the 32-hour vigil, but there were approximately 17 present for the grand entrance. While all of the parents got a chance to briefly visit with Jeri and Wes, none of us were in the room for the actual birth. Wes finally came out briefly around 10:30 p.m. on February 6th and told us that it wouldn't be too much longer.

We were all supposed to stay in the waiting room unless, of course, we needed water or a bathroom break. The water fountain and restroom just happened to be right across the hall from Jeri's room, so Sara (Wes's mom) and I both got thirsty around 11:40 p.m. – right after we saw the doctor go into Jeri's room. We craned our ears and were blessed to hear our granddaughter's first cry – it was 11:52 p.m. – missed my birthday by eight minutes! However, hearing that little cry made up for the early arrival. It was truly one of the highlights of my life. We quickly scooted down the hall back to the waiting room to tell the masses that Baby Brown had indeed arrived!

Shortly after midnight, Wes came out and escorted his parents, Jeri's dad, and me, into their room. It was there that we all met Miss Mackenzie Mara Brown for the very first time. Her eyes were wide open and she appeared to look us each up one side and down the other, probably wondering what in the world she'd gotten herself into. Her middle name is one that Jeri and Wes made up – a combination of my first name (Mary) and Sara's name. That, of course, made Sara and me cry even more.

Mackenzie has six doting grandparents and four doting great-grandparents. She has known all of our names since she first learned to talk and has never mixed any of us up. Considering how close some of the names are, I think that's remarkable – and I'm not at all biased. The names, in alphabetical order are: Grams, Grandma, Grandmamamama (which is really supposed to be Grandmama but once she gets on a roll she can't seem to stop), Nan, Nana (pronounced using the short "a" sound), NaNa (pronounced using the "ah" sound), Pap, Pawpaw, Pop, and Popsaw. Now tell me keeping all those names straight is not monumental!

Considering her grand entrance, I can't wait to see what else Miss Mackenzie has in store for us. With an entrance like hers, the rest of the story is bound to be amazing!

Macyn

I blinked and Mackenzie was no longer the infant of the *grand entrance*.

She and her parents came to eat with us one evening in late November 2006. Mackenzie was wearing a new pink T-shirt, and I was so busy getting supper ready that I didn't really stop to notice the inscription.

"Grams, look at my shirt" she said. And when the words (*I'm the big sister*) registered, I realized she was announcing the impending birth of another Baby Brown. Jeri had done it again – she had come up with another unique way to announce she was pregnant! My heart grew in an instant to include the newest addition to our family.

Another grand entrance adventure had begun, and just as each of us is unique once we arrive on this earth, our journey in the womb is also unique. In January, Mackenzie and her parents went to Disney World – or in Mackenzie's words "Mickey Mouse's Playhouse" for a family vacation with Wes' parents. Jeri didn't ride any dangerous rides, but began experiencing some difficulties. I received the call that no mother wants to get letting me know that Disney World had transported her to the nearest hospital. They discovered that the placenta had shifted positions, and while there was no immediate danger, Jeri should make an appointment to see her doctor once she returned home.

My world stopped while I processed the information I'd just heard, and I fell to my knees and prayed for God to hold us all in His mighty hands. Jeri's doctor confirmed what the doctors in Orlando had said, and for the next several weeks there was some uncertainty as to how everything would turn out.

We were blessed as the placenta righted itself, and the pregnancy continued in the normal way. Soon she and Wes again invested in the handheld monitor, and we were all listening again to the strong heartbeat of the newest little Brown.

As the big day approached, we learned that Jeri had gestation diabetes. She followed the doctor's orders and was able to stay healthy herself, as well as insure the baby's health. In order to insure the baby was a healthy weight, the doctor decided to induce labor on July 6th rather than waiting for the due date of July 20th.

Wes took Mackenzie to school on the 6th, and I picked her up. He and Jeri were to be at the hospital by 7:30 that evening. James drove to my house after he got off work, and Jena met the three of us for supper prior to heading to the hospital.

We arrived at the hospital at the same time Jeri and Wes were walking in. Jena and James took turns entertaining Mackenzie while I tried to appear nonchalant and in control. Matthew had to work late, but came to the hospital as soon as he got off, and Wes' parents rounded out the family vigil committee for that evening.

As midnight approached, we all realized that this Baby Brown was as stubborn as her older sister and wasn't coming a minute before she was ready. The Browns took Mackenzie with them, Matthew went home because he had to work the next morning, and I took James and Jena and we spent the night at Jeri's house.

Bright and early the next morning, James, Jena and I headed back to the hospital to begin the vigil again. In case you've forgotten the date, it was now 07-07-07 – can you believe it! The Browns arrived a little later with Mackenzie, and we all settled in for the wait. Throughout the day family and friends were in and out, and before we knew it most of the same players took their positions for this grand entrance as they had done 3-1/2 years before.

Macyn Michelle Brown was born at 5:12 p.m. that afternoon. Another grand and glorious entrance and as it should have been Mackenzie was the first to see her sister. The rest of us each had our turns, and meeting Macyn for the first time was awesome. It's only been a few months at this writing, but already she has brought more joy to my life than I could have imagined.

I am blessed to be Grams to two beautiful little girls.

But Jesus called them *unto him,* **and said, Suffer little children to come unto me, and forbid them not: for of such is the kingdom of God.** Luke 18:16 (KJV)

Chapter 8
Others Swimming in My Gene Pool
(Their Fingerprints are on My Life)

There are so many swimming in my gene pool we could start our own state – of confusion, that is. Matthew gets a kick out of visiting my relatives because he says he's gathering material for his standup comedy routine in case he's ever selected to be on the television show *Last Comic Standing*.

I'll start with Mother's side of the pool because there are so few of us left. My cousins Karen and Patsy, and me are the only living relatives that knew our grandmother, Rebecca Hogg (Mommy) Steppe. They live near Macon, which is south of Atlanta so we're able to see each other frequently. One of our favorite things to do is meet at Buckner's, a restaurant along I-75, that's a family style, all you can eat, Southern cooking buffet. My mouth is watering and I'm gaining 20 pounds just thinking about it.

Patsy's shopping habits just tickle me to death. She will go to the mall, wandering from store to store asking clerks to hold items because she "just can't decide"; and when she finally makes a decision and purchases something, she immediately begins worrying if it was the right color, the right price, the right who-knows-what. She seems to be in total awe of my and Karen's ability to pick out shoes (for example) instead of agonizing over all the hundreds of choices. Karen and I go to the mall, know exactly what we want, make the purchase and leave. But then there's no suspense or mystery, so maybe Patsy's on to something. Naw, I'm just going to buy the shoes, but shopping with Patsy is an experience to be sure.

While Patsy may anguish over her purchases, Karen and I seem to be magnets for, well, let's just say *unusual* circumstances. We tell ourselves and anyone else who will listen, that we are intelligent women, so every time we end up in one of those circumstances there's a lot of furrowing of the brow, wrinkling of the nose, and scratching of the head.

One day I was driving Karen through various neighborhoods looking for an appropriate house for her to rent. One neighborhood we visited had one main entrance and a thousand (okay, maybe only five) cul-de-sacs. When it was time to leave we could not find the main road out to save our lives. We rode around and around circling around from cul-de-sac to cul-de-sac looking for the escape route. Perhaps we should have left bread crumbs to mark our path. Nothing looked familiar. After thirty minutes or so, we finally found the magic door and escaped. So if you are ever driving along and see two fairly intelligent looking women wandering the highways and by-ways, you might just be following Karen and me. Don't! There's no telling where we will lead you.

Regardless of what Patsy, Karen, and I are up to, being with one another is something we all enjoy. Patsy has had some health issues over the past two years that have made all three of us realize the importance of family, the preciousness of life, and the healing balm of love.

Swimming over to the other side of the pool we find my Dad's relatives. Dad had six brothers and four sisters.

They all married and I've lost count of the in-laws, cousins, 2nd cousins, etc. but I'm sure we're well into three digits. Many of them migrated West and we didn't see them often as I was growing up. Additionally, Mother had issues with some of Dad's relatives, and as a result the relationships were strained even when we were together. There are many relatives I've never met; however, one of my goals is to rectify that situation and get to know them. It's a daunting task, but with modern technology, and grown kids who know how to surf the internet, it's a task I'm ready to attempt. There is, however, a core group of Barringtons that I do know, and while I can't mention them all here because there isn't enough ink or paper, I want to introduce you to a few of them who have helped shape me into who I am.

I have hero-worshipped my Aunt Lois for as long as I remember. She's one of Dad's younger sisters and since she's only 11 years older than me, she didn't want me calling her *aunt*, so we're more like sisters than aunt/niece. She became a single mom about a year or so before I did and she was always there for me during my struggles as a single mom. Spending time with her is a breath of fresh air for me. She is one of the easiest people to be around and she has taught me so much about life – especially how to roll with the punches. No matter what life throws at her, she continues on her journey being the pleasant, wonderful lady that she is.

Dad's youngest sister is Debbie, and since I'm named for her she was always "big Debbie" and I was "little Debi" – kind of like *The Waltons*. She's 4 years older than me and I followed her around like a sick puppy. I'm sure she must have gotten tired of it, but she never complained about it and always made me feel special. I wish someone had made a home movie the day she was teaching me the *twist* after Chubby Checker made his recording, because it is a cherished memory from my childhood.

Grace is a cousin who lives in Pensacola. I recently met her, her husband, and her brother's wife, Patti, at the Albuquerque airport. We all piled into the rental car and proceeded to take thirty minutes trying to find our way out of the airport parking area, even making one pass through the *long term* parking deck. We were actually on what we thought was the highway two different times before meandering back into the parking lot. We saw our hotels over the retaining wall but we couldn't get to them. I kept looking to see if Karen was in the car with us, but then to my utter horror realized that I was the common denominator. *I'm* directionally challenged and apparently cause all those around me to suffer from it as well. Aside from our adventure in NM, Grace and Erich (her husband) have taught me to slow down and embrace the moment. They've taught me to stop hurrying and scurrying about as I tend to do, and really relax and let life take me wherever it may.

Uncle Paul was one of Dad's younger brothers. He had already left the Pensacola area by the time I was in elementary school, so I didn't see him that often as a child. However, as an adult he and I cultivated a relationship that I'm sure evolved from the fact that we both like to march to our own drummer – and we respected that in each other. He was a Baptist minister for many years, before he felt lead to become a Methodist minister. He was the logical one to call when I felt lead to the Methodist Church because he was the one person I knew who would understand what I was experiencing at the time. As I was completing this book, Uncle Paul lost his battle with cancer. When I think of him, I hear his laughter, I hear his many stories, and I treasure the times we were together. One early morning on a family fishing trip in 1999, he took me out in his boat to his "hot" spot in the lake, and with his instruction I caught more fish on that morning than I had in my whole life before that day. I will never forget that morning, and the lessons that I've learned from Uncle Paul.

Aunt Helen is married to my Uncle Gene. They also left the Pensacola area, and with the exception of the time they visited us when I was 12 years old, I didn't really see them until I became an adult. By that time their daughters were also adults, living their own lives and their son was a teenager, who only came East with them once that I recall. I'm so blessed that as an adult I got to know Aunt Helen and Uncle Gene, because each of them has enriched my life. Their faith in God is an example for all of us to strive for. And until just recently when she was stricken with leukemia, Aunt Helen was always working in the yard – always busy, never lazy. One of my fondest memories of her is riding the tractor, cutting her grass in 2005 when Dad and I visited with them in OK – she was in her 80's. I hope to be just like her when I'm in my 80's. She and Uncle Gene have dealt with his failing health since 1998. She just recently learned that she has acute leukemia and her time on this earth is short – and yet their faith has not failed.

Dad's family roots are in Ohio. In 1926 my grandfather decided to move his family to Pensacola, FL. I'm not sure why, they didn't keep in touch with the Ohio branch of relatives through the years, but for some reason they didn't. It was a pleasant surprise to learn about my cousin Chris from Ohio – yes, my Yankee cousin, Chris. We began our relationship via e-mail and learned that we shared a love for the book and movie *Gone With the Wind*. She flew to Atlanta to not only meet me, but also to visit the Margaret Mitchell Museum and the National Cemetery in Marietta where our ancestor, Charles Springer, who was killed during the Civil War is buried. Grace also came up that weekend, and the three of us roamed the streets of Atlanta enjoying the museums, the historical battlefields, and the food (Chris liked the fried green tomatoes but wasn't thrilled with the turnip greens). When we weren't exploring graveyards, battlefields or old apartments where famous authors once lived, we were getting to know each other. The conversation was easy and the joys and laughs were many. Chris and I maintain our long distance relationship by staying in touch via e-mail, snail mail, and phone calls. Even though we've only met once, the closeness is there and it is a most precious thing.

It was very surreal visiting the grave of Charles Springer that weekend. I knew I had relatives that fought on both sides during that war, but as I visited his grave the reality of the horrors of that war truly sank in. Since my subdivision is near some of the battle fields, I sometimes sit on my deck at night and visualize the soldiers in both the blue and gray as they marched through the woods near my house. My Dad has the diary carried by his great-grandfather, Jeroboam Baer Creighton, who was in the Union Army and fought in *The Battle of Atlanta*. I've read the diary since moving to the Atlanta area, and it's truly a moving piece of literature. Standing at Charles' grave, remembering the passages from that diary, I experienced a revelation about the war itself that I'd never understood before. I came to realize that it was a war that needed to be fought from a *state's right* perspective, but I also realized that the Union had to ultimately win to preserve the freedom's we all covet. For this girl who's a card carrying G.R.I.T.S. (girl raised in the South) that was profound.

No matter which side of the gene pool I'm swimming in, my life is touched and usually blessed. I say usually, because my family, like everyone else's isn't perfect. We have our moments. We sometimes say or do hurtful things to one another. We sometimes get on each other's nerves. We sometimes don't understand each other. But at the end of the day, when all is said and done, it comes down to the fact that we are family and the bond of love will not be broken – no matter what.

The purpose of this chapter was not only to introduce you to some of my relatives who've made a difference in my life, but also to help you stop and consider the relatives you have that have made a difference in your life. Maybe it's time to put down the book and send an e-mail, write a letter, or make a phone call.

Chapter 9
The Blues Sisters

I am blessed with three best friends – Matthew, Jeri, and Iris. I depend on each of them to keep me centered, true to myself and on track in life. They each have their own role to play in my life and all of them play it well.

I've already told you about Matthew and Jeri, so now I'll introduce you to Iris Mills Broadbent. For many years she lived in the Chicago area and even though there were 700 miles (give or take a mile) from driveway to driveway, we were still close and were still there for each other, if not always in body at least in spirit. She recently moved to South Carolina and is only 207.3 miles away (but who's counting?). We're definitely going to make up for lost time now that she's so close. We talk on the phone frequently and occasionally one of us shocks the other and actually sends a card or letter. Prior to meeting Matthew, Iris was my soul mate. One of my friends actually described Matthew as the male version of Iris.

Iris is a once in a lifetime type of friend – one to whom you can say anything without fearing judgment; the person you call in the middle of the night when you're having a panic attack and you'll know she'll listen and not complain that you've called so late. There is no façade. There is no window dressing. Pure honesty – sometimes brutally so – but never meant to hurt, always meant to help.

I don't think either of us knows exactly how or when we became friends; it just happened. We met for the first time in early 1984. She was the pastor's wife at the church we joined after moving to Georgia. By 1988 we were best friends.

One of the reasons we clicked so well and so quickly, is that we had walked a similar road to get to where we were in life. Both of us suffered from varying degrees of self-esteem issues and we were trying to work through those.

The two of us have been through many things together, including rolling a car – and living to tell about it, sitting in hospital waiting rooms with each other, supporting one another as the other's marriage crumbled and praying over the phone with each other when being there in person just wasn't possible.

We set a goal to have at least one girl's weekend a year. Our very first trip was several years ago when Iris got the bright idea to go river rafting. There were seven rafts in all – one in the front with a guide, two behind that one, a middle one with a guide, two more behind that one, and a sweeper (final) raft with a guide (that's the one that *swept* anyone who fell out of the other six). We (I) made sure we were in a raft with a guide and we ended up in the sweeper raft. Initially the trip was peaceful and tranquil. We were enjoying Nature as we slowly made our way down the river. As we approached the BIG (did I say BIG?) rapids, all seven rafts pulled over to the side. The three guides led us to the top of a cliff overlooking the rapids so we could see from on high just where we'd be going. One look was all I needed to realize that I'd be the person who held anyone else's glasses, hats, and anything else they wanted held. Iris said, "If you don't go, you'll regret it the rest of your life." I knew if I went there'd be no *rest of my life*. Iris has a picture from that trip. I don't, because the only official shot was of the rafts going OVER the big rapids – no picture of the glasses and hat holder standing on the cliff. Oh well, I have my life.

Sometimes it takes a best friend to speak the truth as no one else can. While visiting an antique store in Blue Island, IL, with Iris I made the comment, "These aren't antiques. We used to have some of these same things when I was growing up." Iris then eloquently pointed out that WE'RE ANTIQUES! ARGH!!!!!!!!!

Once we disguised ourselves (sunglasses and hats) and headed to a church that was thinking about calling her husband as its pastor. We had to check it out, and they'd met her so she couldn't just waltz in there. We looked like the *Blues Sisters* which became our nickname after that excursion.

The most precious aspect of our relationship is our honesty. We love one another too much to settle for anything less. We don't let the other one get away with anything. We keep each other centered and anchored. We're not identical and at times have rather lively discussions; but we're in tune with one another enough to cut through the bull and get to the meat of the matter. I have learned acceptance, compassion, and unconditional love from Iris.

Everyone needs a friend like Iris. Everyone should be a friend like Iris.

Proverbs 17:17a – **A friend loveth at all times.** (KJV)

PART THREE

Dancing Like No One is Watching

You've met me and you've met some of my family members and friends. Now curl up with a nice drink and meet some of my thoughts and ideas, which will ultimately lead you to meet my Lord as we continue to dance through the rest of my garage.

Chapter 1
Always Look to Make Sure There Isn't a Frog in Your Toilet

As we go through life, we often leap before we look – or at least I find that to be true in my life. Sometimes, I suppose it's because we think that we have all the facts when, in reality, we only have part of the facts. Or perhaps, it's something that we want so badly we really don't want to know all the facts because if we really knew the facts, we'd use our better judgment and not do it.

Matthew found an example of this in a most unusual place – the hall bathroom of our house, also known as the *reading room* in some circles. One night in the wee hours of the morning he got up to visit the reading room. As was his custom, he turned on the light so he could see.

What to his wondering eyes should appear? A FROG! It was in our toilet. Yes, a real, live frog peering up at Matthew as if to say "Hey buddy, why'd you turn on the light? I'm trying to sleep here!"

Of course, Matthew yelled for me to come. He ran and got the digital camera because no one would believe this otherwise. There we stood in our hall bathroom in the middle of the night with a frog in our toilet as the subject of our photo shoot.

After the photo shoot, we had to figure out how to help Mr. Frog out of our bathroom and out of the house.

We (Matthew) somehow coaxed him into a plastic cup and took him outside to live happily in the grass and hop away to his life's content.

To this day it is a mystery as to how he got in the toilet in the first place, but you can rest assured that on my nightly visits to the reading room I now flip the light on to make sure he hasn't decided to make an encore.

The same should be true of decisions we face in life. Flip the switch and be sure there isn't something uninvited awaiting you before you leap. Talk to God and get His take on the situation before you make a decision.

Proverbs 3:5 – **Trust in the Lord with all thine heart; and lean not unto thine own understanding.** (KJV)

Chapter 2
To Thine Own Self Be True – I'm Working on It

Many times we may ask ourselves, "Why am I here?" or "What is my purpose?" or "What can I do to improve my world?"

The best way to answer these questions is to be honest with your own self – *to thine own self be true*. When we find ourselves in certain situations, in certain arenas, we have to explore the reason or reasons we are there. If the reasons are very clear and very deliberate, then fine, that's where we should be at that particular time. On the other hand, if the reasons are hazy, if we can't put our finger on exactly why we do what we do, then perhaps it's time to change direction and do something else.

I have changed directions a few times in my life. In June of 1983, I traveled from Hanahan to Atlanta for my sister Jo Ellen's wedding. Driving home, my husband commented that he wished we lived in the Atlanta area. We'd been talking about moving for years so I finally said, "If that's what we really want – then let's do it!" And we did! We were living in Atlanta three months later. What seemed like a spur of the moment move by outsiders looking in was, in reality, a dream we'd had for a long time. We'd just never taken any action to make the dream a reality.

Once we began acting on our dreams, things literally fell into place for us. The For Sale sign went up on Monday and our house in Hanahan sold by Friday of the same week. We found a place near Atlanta to live. It was something really wonderful to experience. We had a true peace that we were where we were supposed to be, doing what we were supposed to do. It was one of those moments in life when we KNEW beyond a shadow of a doubt that we'd made the right choice. Had I not gone through the *Atlanta* door when it opened, my life would have turned out very differently.

I'm venturing through another open door as I complete this manuscript. I have dreamt of being a writer since I was 13 years old but I was always afraid to *act* on that dream for fear of failure. I made a few timid attempts during my first two years of high school, but was told by both my mother and the journalism teacher that I had no talent. So I put my tablet away and didn't pick it up again for almost 30 years. The point is I REALLY WANT TO BE A WRITER and I wasn't true to myself. I let other people squash my dream. When Matthew came into my life he began to encourage me to write a book so, with his encouragement, I began to stoke the writing embers that were deep within my soul.

Hand in hand with writing is also a dream to speak and share the lessons I've learned and the blessings I've received as I've chartered the course through the waters of my life.

In order to be true to myself and to make both of these dreams become my reality I had to take action. I took classes, I read books, I joined Toastmasters and a speaker's workshop and I found a mentor.

I began seeking opportunities to speak and those opportunities became realities at churches, at schools, and at civic groups. Then I had to overcome my biggest obstacle – setting aside time to write the book. So for the past several months, I've been in my office night after night, determined to complete this book. Poor Matthew has been a real trouper as he bore the burden of most of the housework, meals, etc., as I would come home from work and head to the office to write.

I actually thought I'd finished the book in the fall of 2005 and even sent out query letters; however, I didn't get a single nibble. I know now it wasn't God's will for that book to be published because it has undergone a major metamorphosis as God as spoken to me time and time again during these many months since then.

At one time in my life, I would have given up completely when no one responded to my query letters, thus ending my dream. But I have learned that if you want something badly enough you must be willing to give it your all and not give up when obstacles arise.

As I began to walk these new avenues in the writing/speaking territory, I was floundering and waffling as to who my target audience would be. I knew what I wanted to say. I just couldn't figure out who I wanted to say it to. I know now that's why the book kept evolving – I was still looking for my audience. God knew who my audience was all along. He'd been prodding me to become a Christian speaker but I'd been fighting that idea, telling Him that, "I'd be a speaker who was a Christian, but that I didn't want to be a Christian speaker".

I stopped running from God's plan last year at a women's retreat that was sponsored by my church. The speaker that weekend was Cathy Lee Phillips. One morning at breakfast I mentioned to her that she was living the life I wanted to live. She made several suggestions to me that weekend, helping me to overcome the fear I had of yielding to God's will to be a Christian speaker. She has become my mentor and as a result of her guidance, I'm in the will of God for my life, the words are flowing again and I've found my target audience.

I'm still a work in progress with regard to being true to myself and allowing God to lead me on the paths that He has chosen for me. I'm holding onto God's hand as He leads me through the doors He is opening. If I'm true to Him and true to myself, my dreams will become my reality.

Being true to oneself is not a small task, but a task worth undertaking. As you read this, ask God what changes you might need to make in your life in order to meet the real you and be true to yourself. Considering that He created us, it stands to reason that He knows what is best for us. He knows what our talents are and He's not going to lead us to do something that we'll be miserable doing. He loves us and will guide us in our search for ourselves.

Proverbs 3:6 – **In all thy ways acknowledge him, and he shall direct thy paths.** (KJV)

Chapter 3
Who's In Charge?

Have you ever felt that your life is totally out of your control and you are just spinning around and around and getting nowhere fast? Who's in control of your life? What would it take for you to regain the reigns of your life?

I struggle with this time to time because I have a habit of occasionally allowing my life to run ahead of me. It tends to slip up on me as I include first one thing and then another and another into my already tight schedule and before I know it, I'm spinning out of control. So what is the answer? How do I take charge?

First of all, I have to own up to the fact that my life – I'll repeat that – MY LIFE, is what I have made it. Secondly, I take a deep breath and try to step back from the madness long enough to remember what my original goals were. Thirdly, I re-evaluate my priorities, trying to reorganize my life and turning down the volume in order to get things on a more even keel – considering what things to keep and what things to discard. Fourthly, and most importantly, I seek God's guidance.

There are so many wonderful causes for which we can volunteer, excellent organizations that we can join, classes that we can take, parties that we can attend – and if we did them all, we would be busy constantly. God didn't intend for us to always be on the go and never rest. He set the example by resting on the seventh day of creation. I have a tendency to fill my schedule too full.

I've realized that sometimes I can't make it to every meeting. Sometimes I just need a night off. I'm learning to say NO when I need to and not feel guilty. I'm learning that just because I choose not to do something doesn't mean I'm not committed to the cause – it just means that I can't do that particular thing on that particular day. There always seems to be one or two in every group that try to make me feel guilty for saying no. They can't make me feel guilty because I'm in charge of my reaction to their comments and therefore in charge of my feelings.

There are other times in my life when things just don't go as planned. I've learned not to react to the situation – and I'm getting better about remembering that lesson (I really am). Nuclear explosions are called *reactions* for a reason. There was a time in my life that I'm sure some of my friends wanted to nickname me *Atomic* or something similar, because I had the terrible habit of over-reacting. I've learned to step back from the situation and not just react to it. Life happens and mistakes are made. Sometimes it isn't even a mistake – it's just the way things are. Like Atlanta traffic. No matter how well I plan my travel time, an accident or just the sheer volume of cars will invariably slow me down to a crawl and I'll be late. I have two choices: 1) I can sulk/fume/scream or 2) I can take it in stride. I've learned to take it in stride – most of the time. Some days are hectic at work – I've learned (okay, I'm learning) to take those days in stride.

I've learned to set aside time to rest and relax. Matthew and I have created a very tranquil and peaceful area on and around our deck. There are plants, bird feeders, a swing, lanterns, Christmas lights (yes, we're rednecks) and all the things we enjoy as we sit out there early in the morning or late in the evening. It's a time to unwind and allow God to recharge us.

When life starts coming at you from all sides and you feel yourself losing control, remember these four things: 1) take ownership of the choices you made that propelled you to where you are; 2) take a deep breath and remember what your original goals were; 3) re-evaluate your priorities; and, most importantly, 4) seek God's guidance. He promises to be with us always and that includes the *out of control* times of our lives. He'll help you regain control and be in charge of your life. Matthew 28:20b **And, lo, I am with you alway,** *even* **unto the end of the world. A-men.** (KJV)

Chapter 4
Life's a Baseball Game, Swing That Bat!

I'm standing there staring the pitcher down. I'm ready. I'm gonna knock one over the fence. It's been a good year. Yes sir, it's been a very good year, so I'm ready for the pitch.

I stare at the pitcher – the pitcher stares at me. I dig in – the pitcher plants. I wave the bat – the pitcher winds up. I'm ready. Here comes the ball. Swishshshshshsh

What in the world was that?

Ok – I'm ready now. I stare at the pitcher – the pitcher stares at me. I dig in – the pitcher plants. I wave the bat – the pitcher winds up. I'm ready. Here comes the ball. Swishshshshshsh

Good grief. I ask for time out and step out of the batter's box. That was the fastest, meanest curve ball I've ever seen. Wow, this pitcher is tricky. Then I remember, oh yeah, the pitcher is *Life*. And *Life* just threw me a curve.

The umpire is about to say, "Batter up," again so I'm taking a few practice swings. I'm trying to plot some strategy to win this game of life. We never know when *Life* is going to zing that nasty curve ball right at us. We don't always see it coming – actually, we rarely see it coming. *Life* is good with that curve ball.

The key to dealing with that pitch is not to let one pitch take you out of the game. The game of life isn't made up of just that one pitch. Don't get so caught up on hitting the curve ball that you miss the soft lob coming at you. Realize also that you **can** handle a curve if you have to. Don't be afraid to get back in that batter's box. You don't have to knock it out of the park every time; just try and get on base. That's all you have to do.

"BATTER UP!" cries the umpire.

Okay, one quick swig of water, one quick search of the crowd to find my family cheering me on and it is back to the batter's box.

I do what I've heard Babe Ruth did years ago; I point to where my ball will go. I **know** I'm going to hit it this time. It may not go out of the park, but I **will get a hit.**

I stare at the pitcher – the pitcher stares at me. I dig in – the pitcher plants. I wave the bat – the pitcher winds up. I'm ready. Here comes the ball.

SMACCKCKKCKCKCKCKCK. I did it, I did it – I got a hit, I got a hit. Good grief, you mean I've got to **run** to first base now?

2 Timothy 4:7 – **I have fought a good fight, I have finished my course, I have kept the faith.** (KJV)

I wish I could say I always practiced what I preach, but I don't. I apparently have the same problem St. Paul had. **I do not understand what I do. For what I want to do I do not do, but what I hate I do.** Romans 15:7 (NIV)

There are times when I panic over the least little thing! Occasionally something as simple as misplacing a sheet of paper, can push me to the edge. I'm constantly working with myself because it's usually not the big things that bother me, it's the little things that drive me nuts. And in the scheme of life, they're just not even on the radar screen and my reaction is out of proportion for the circumstances. I keep saying God's not finished with me yet – and He's not. I'm certain that He will continue to mold me into the person He created me to be. Isaiah 64:8 – **But now, O Lord, thou *art* our father; we *are* the clay, and thou our potter; and we all *are* the work of thy hand.** (KJV)

Chapter 5
Is This The Number to Whom I'm Speaking?

I had one of the weirdest phone experiences of my life one day when I was trying to cancel a magazine subscription that I knew I hadn't renewed even though the address label showed the expiration date to be the following year. I dialed the 1-800 number to tell them I hadn't renewed the subscription. I was told by the man on the other end that my subscription had been renewed through a third party billing process and would have to call another 1-800 number. I dialed the second number, ready to explain to whomever answered that I had not renewed the subscription; however, the phone wasn't answered by a human and the conversation (and I used that word very loosely) went something like this:

"Welcome to the magazine subscription hot line. If you would like to place a new subscription say 'new,' if you would like to cancel an existing subscription say 'cancel.'"

"Cancel"

"OK – I'll try to help you with that. What credit card did you use to place your subscription?"

"I don't know. I didn't place a subscription."

"I'm sorry, I did not understand what you said. Please say something like 'VISA,' 'MASTER CARD,' 'DISCOVER' or 'AMERICAN EXPRESS.'"

"I don't know – I didn't authorize a renewal!"

"I don't know why I am having so much trouble helping you. Let's try another approach. What is your last name? Say it very slowly."

"MER—CHANT."

"Let me repeat that back to you, MER—CHANT. Is that correct?"

"Yes."

"Would you please spell that for me – letter by letter?" (like there's any other way to spell something?)

"M E R C H A N T."

"Let me repeat that back to you, M E R C H A N T. Is that correct?"

"Yes."

"OK – I have your records now. Please say the name of the magazine you'd like to cancel."

"Soap Opera Digest."

"OK – I see that subscription. Did you know that I can give you another year of that magazine for 25% off what you're currently paying and if you decide to do this, I can send you a stainless steel coffee travel mug? Would you like for me to do that now?"

"No."

"I'm sorry that I can't help you get your travel mug. Are you sure you don't want the mug?"

"I'm sure – just cancel the subscription."

"OK – I have canceled your subscription – your cancellation number is 555555. Please call again if the magazine subscription hot line can be of further service to you."

And I didn't exaggerate. It really happened, just like that!

Now what on earth is the lesson in this little story? It is: *Don't take life so seriously.* There will be days when not only computers but also people will not understand you and you won't understand them. Just realize these days are part of life and, for goodness sake, laugh!

Chapter 6
Through Their Eyes

Think of the first time you saw cotton candy. Or the first time you saw the ocean. Or the first time you saw a rose. Are you able to relive the moments? Did you feel the excitement of the **first** time? Have you ever taken the time to watch a young child experience something for the **first** time?

The smallest things can bring such excitement to them. If we could just see the world through their eyes, everything would be exciting. Everything would be amazing!

I saw the world anew in my twenties through the eyes of my children and now, in my fifties, I'm seeing it anew through the eyes of my granddaughters.

One of my most cherished home videos is one James made when he was about nine. He was filming any and everything that day. As you view the video you see trees, you see family members, you see pets and you see the garden. An adult may have stopped filming at that point, but not James. He noticed a ladybug on one of the leaves in the garden. Since he didn't know how to zoom in and out, he actually moved the camera to zoom in on the ladybug. It's an incredible shot and his commentary is priceless. As we were about to go in that day, James noticed a garter snake slithering across the yard. He filmed the entire trek of the snake, giving commentary such as, "It's a snake," and, "Oh my gosh!" and, "Would you look at that?" and simply, "Wow." I, on the other hand, ran for my life! But James saw the beauty. He saw the wonder.

I'm glad I'm getting another chance to view the world through the eyes of a child. Mackenzie and Macyn explore their world daily and see and learn new and exciting things that we adults take for granted.

Several months ago Mackenzie was at our house and realized the automatic night-light in the hallway would come on when she walked passed it and blocked the light. You should have seen the look on her face as she began to process this information. She called herself *Mimi* at the time and she was standing there saying, "Mimi did it! Mimi did it!" She kept taking her finger and covering the sensor to make the light come on over and over again. It was the wonder of it all to her. It was exciting and amazing to her and her excitement was so contagious that I was amazed as well.

If we could bottle that aspect of our personality so we could keep it even as adults, just think how awesome our lives would be. We'd take nothing for granted. Everything would be exciting and amazing. Everything would be filled with wonder.

This isn't a new idea. Jesus spoke of it when He walked among us. Mark 10:15 – **Verily I say unto you, Whosoever shall not receive the kingdom of God as a little child, he shall not enter therein.** (KJV)

That means seeing the kingdom of God through the eyes of a child. It means experiencing the kingdom of God with the same wonder as James videotaping a ladybug or Mackenzie standing in the hallway making an automatic night-light go on and off.

In order to fully appreciate life, we must become childlike to the extent that we're willing to be empty vessels to be filled. Filled with excitement. Filled with amazement. Filled with wonder. Filled with life.

Chapter 7
No Time Like the Present

Time waits for no man

There's never enough time

Time is running out

Do you get the feeling we're obsessed with time? Many of us feel we need more time. What do we do with our time? How do we spend our time?

Do we waste time? Or do we fill every waking hour of our time running around to various meetings and working on various projects?

I fall into the last category. I spend so much time running around doing all these extra curricular activities, sometimes the things that are truly important get left undone or unattended like:

Matthew: I'm working so fast and furiously during the day at work, many days I just come home so tired that I practically fall asleep during supper.

Mackenzie: On a recent day off, I planned to pick her up from school for some quality time – but I was so busy doing housework, running errands, etc., that I ended up with barely 30 minutes to spend with her.

A friend from high school: He was battling cancer for about two years. He died before I got to Charleston to visit him, even though I knew he was sick. I kept planning to go – someday...

Do these scenarios sound familiar to you? Do any of them strike a chord in your life?

What's the answer? We have to work. We have to do chores. We need to be involved with good causes in our community. We can't visit all of our friends all of the time. So how do we solve this dilemma?

I've been thinking about this since my friend's death, and I've come up with some changes that I'm making in my life.

1) I've decided not to give myself a heart attack over the work in the office. The work will be done, but I'll set priorities and stop hopping from one thing to another in such a frantic state that I drain myself completely and have nothing left when I get home. I'm setting aside at least one night a week as mine and Matthew's night. Short of an extreme emergency nothing will pre-empt our plans. We may choose to see a movie, eat out, go for a walk, or just sit on the deck and enjoy each other's company. What we do isn't important; doing it together is important.

2) When I pick up Mackenzie and Macyn from school, I'll be there early enough so we can spend some quality time together. Even at just 3-1/2 years old, Mackenzie has developed a passion for Starbucks coffee and having coffee there has become one of

our rituals. She sits there drinking her White Chocolate Mocha (no fat, no whip) just like a big girl – in fact, she has her own Starbucks cup. Even though Macyn is only a few months old, I'm sure she and I will also develop our own rituals. I'm committed to being a Grams that has time for them. It doesn't matter what we do, as long as we do it.

3) I have friends and family spread all over the country. Seeing each of them every year would be impossible due to my schedule as well as their schedules; however, I'm going to make plans to visit and stay in touch with as many of them as I possibly can. Within the past several months, I've made trips to SC, NM, OK, and FL reconnecting with family and friends. Three of my classmates from Hanahan (Marilyn, Gail, and Cindy) settled in the Jacksonville area, and we manage to get together every other year for our own version of the *YaYa Sisters*. I'm not letting another friend or family member die without my stopping long enough to cherish our relationship. A short e-mail, a short phone call, a short note – just to say "hi, I'm thinking of you".

Those are my plans. I challenge you to set priorities so that time doesn't get away from you. After all, there's no time like the present.

Romans 13:11 – **And do this, understanding the present time. The hour has come for you to wake up from your slumber, because our salvation is nearer now than when we first believed. (NIV)**

Chapter 8
Pray Without Ceasing

Some people think of God as a celestial Santa Claus. I'm not one of them. However, I do believe He is concerned and interested in all we do, even the little things. For instance, when I was a teenager my cat wandered off as cats will do. He was gone for several days. I remember praying during a Wednesday night prayer service at church that he would come home. Believe it or not, there he was sitting on the back stoop when we drove into the carport.

Another time I'll never forget is the time I lost my grandmother's diamond ring at the softball field. I was the third generation to wear the ring. I was on the ladies softball team at my church and we had been practicing that afternoon. Somehow, the person holding my rings had dropped that one and it was nowhere to be found. The following morning, my husband went back to the ball field to look for it with a metal detector. It was about that time that I realized how much the ring meant to me. It was the only tangible thing I had from my mother's side of the family. So, I got on my knees to pray. Right before I closed my eyes I saw Jeri's stuffed bear, with his mouth hanging off to one side, right where I had put it after she brought it to me to repair. As I began to pray, I heard God speak to me. He told me that my ring was no more important to Him than Jeri's bear's mouth was to me. I immediately got up and repaired the bear's mouth. I looked at my digital clock radio – it was 7:45 a.m. A few minutes later my husband walked in with the ring. He'd found it in the dugout. When I asked him what time, he responded, "About 7:45."

God ALWAYS answers prayer, but I learned many years ago that God has three answers: yes, no, and wait. Sometimes we forget that *no* and *wait* are answers. Sometimes we forget that God knows best and since we can't see the whole picture, we only *think* we need certain things. He knows that's not what we need at all. As we pray and commune with our God, let's trust Him to meet our needs in His time.

God wants us to commune with Him. He wants to be asked to participate in our lives. He wants to bless us. Prayer is one of the vehicles for this communication. Take advantage of it. Commune with your God. He's only a prayer away.

Matthew 6:8b – **For your Father knows what you need before you ask Him.** (NIV)

Chapter 9
You Can't Judge a Book by Its Cover

Once I received a book that had a beautiful red cover. It was soft leather and the title, *Everything I Know About Raising Kids*, was intriguing because I had two small children and needed all the guidance I could get. I opened the book and what do you suppose I found? I found blank page after blank page. It was a joke that my friend had found in the bookstore and thought I'd get a kick out of it. I did get a good laugh, but it also brought to mind that great truth – you can't judge a book by its cover.

Not only are we unable to judge books by their covers, we can't judge people by what we see on the outside because sometimes what we think we see is not really what we saw at all.

Consider the story of the four blind men who are taken to the circus for the very first time. They are allowed to touch the elephant. The first man touches the elephant's trunk. The second man touches the elephant's side. The third man touches the elephant's massive leg. The fourth man touches the elephant's tail. On the way home the men are discussing their experiences and the first one comments, "I never realized before that elephants were hoses."

"They aren't hoses," says the second, "they are huge walls".

The third man argues, "You're both wrong; elephants are pillars."

The fourth man insists that all of the other three are wrong because, "Elephants are ropes."

Each man only had a portion of the truth. With his limited ability, each was unable to grasp the entire truth. That's the same thing we encounter when we try to judge another person. We don't know the whole story. We can't grasp the entire truth. We don't have all the facts, so there's no way that we can with a certainty judge the actions of others. We can't ever honestly say, "I know what I'd do in that situation," because we've never been **in that situation, carrying the same baggage as the person we're judging!** We can say what we *think* we would do or what we *hope* we would do – but not what we WOULD do!

This concept came roaring home to me in 1990 when I divorced. To set the stage, let's go back a few years. I'd been brought up in a very strict Southern Baptist home – no dancing, no drinking, and certainly no divorcing. I was such a pious little Christian, I thought I had all the answers. I thought the sermons were preached for others in the congregation rather than to me. And then reality set in – my marriage came tumbling down around me. Divorce was not just an easy decision. I prayed long and hard before filing for divorce. It was one of the most difficult decisions I've ever made.

Imagine my shock when a handful of my friends began to judge me for my decision. What in the world? They knew me. Surely they knew that I'd prayed about it.

How dare they judge me? And then it hit me – I was just as guilty of judging other people all those years before.

For the first time, I began to understand Matthew 7:1-2. **Do not judge, or you too will be judged. For in the same way you judge others, you will be judged, and with the measure you use, it will be measured to you.** (NIV) The measure is the human yardstick. We humans have no way of seeing the entire picture the way God does. We as humans are incapable of making fair judgments because we don't have ALL the facts. We're not able to see all the underlying currents that cause people to act in certain ways. One year, Jeri's Math book actually had one or two word problems whose answer was "un-solvable - not enough facts."

That's the way we need to approach our judgments of other people. I've come to realize that what matters is not what other people think of me but rather what I think of myself, and what I believe God is saying to me. I've learned to appreciate the uniqueness of other people and to accept them for who they are without judging them.

Sometimes it's hard not to judge. We see someone do a certain thing or act a certain way or dress a certain way and we have a tendency to pass judgment. Even though I've learned this isn't right, I still struggle with it. But I know God isn't finished with me yet and I know I can trust Him to forgive me, re-mold the clay of my life, and fashion me into the person He created me to be. The challenge is realizing we're all human and we all do things someone wants to judge. Only God has that wisdom and only God can forgive us when we succumb to the temptation to judge a fellow traveler.

Chapter 10
Four P's in 2007's Pod

I'm not sure about the rest of the country, but on January 1st a Southerner's menu includes collard greens, cornbread, and black eye peas. Hold that thought.

I've decided to stop using the term *New Year's Resolutions*. As a child I used to call them *revolutions*, and as an adult when it came to my weight issues, that came closer to the truth every January 1st as I began again the **Battle Of My Bulge**.

Now, back to the peas...this year – 2007 – will be different for me. This year I'm committed to move forward in my journey of self-development and a healthier me. And since I don't do resolutions anymore, my theme for 2007 is *Four P's in 2007's Pod*.

I've been actively involved in church since I was two weeks old – and that's a LONG, LONG time. But it still amazes me how God works His magic and His wonder in our lives. I had picked my New Year's theme prior to reading my Sunday School lesson and, lo and behold, the first lesson of the New Year related to me.

We were studying the book *The Life You've Always Wanted* by John Ortberg. Would you believe that the first chapter was about transformation? Would you believe that I felt God speaking to me not only as I read the lesson before class, but also as it was being taught? Well, of course you would, because you know that once we turn our lives over to God – He works in us!

Transformation for me involves four P's that are now in my pod:

PRAYER – PROMISES – PROGRESS – PRAISE

Prayer is as vital to our spiritual life as food is to our physical life. Jesus is our example. He is the Son of God, and He began the day with prayer. Mark 1:35 –**Very early in the morning, while it was still dark, Jesus got up, left the house and went off to a solitary place, where he prayed.** (NIV)

Sometimes God's answers to my prayers are *WOW moments*. One of those moments happened in early 1981 when I was the mother of a three-year old and an infant. It seemed the only place I could have any privacy was the bathroom. One Saturday evening I went into the bathroom to have my devotion in peace and quiet. The Scripture was Isaiah 40:31 – **but those who hope in the Lord will renew their strength, They will soar on wings like eagles; they will run and not grow weary, they will walk and not be faint.** (NIV)

After I read it, I prayed that God would make that verse come alive for me. Did I say it was a Saturday night? The text for Sunday morning's message was – you guessed it – Isaiah 40:31! And the pastor made it come so alive for me that it is now my favorite passage. God hears our prayers and He answers them

God's *promises* are available to all of us. He is always with us – we just have to reach for His hand to receive His help and His power.

God has been with me through everything I've ever endured – two major surgeries as a young child, deaths of family members including my mother, the death of my first marriage – the list is endless. It's endless because His presence in our lives is endless.

There have been many times in my life when I literally pictured myself climbing up into this huge rocking chair and God holding me, soothing me and rocking me in His loving arms. His presence was that real to me. I was in His lap. He is faithful. He will never leave us. **Know therefore that the Lord your God is God; he is the faithful God, keeping his covenant of love to a thousand generations of those who love him and keep his commands.** Deuteronomy 7:9 (NIV)

Through *prayer* and because of God's *promises* we will make *progress*. Philippians 3:13 – **Brothers, I do not consider myself yet to have taken hold of it. But one thing I do: Forgetting what is behind and straining toward what is ahead.** (NIV)

My challenge at the moment is to forget my 2006 Weight Watcher's year. I was less than two pounds from goal on April 30, 2006, and yet due to my poor choices I regained what I had lost and as of December 30, 2006, was more than 15 pounds from goal. I was teary-eyed at my meeting that day and the facilitator put her arms around me and said, "2006 is the past; 2007 is your future."

Doesn't that sound like the Philippians 3:13? With God's help, I will put 2006 behind me, begin making healthy choices again and get back on track.

Remember the 10 lepers that Jesus healed? The story is found in Luke 17:11-16 – **Now on his way to Jerusalem, Jesus traveled along the border between Samaria and Galilee. As he was going into a village, ten men who had leprosy met him. They stood at a distance and called out in a loud voice, "Jesus, Master, have pity on us!" When he saw them, he said, "Go, show yourselves to the priests." And as they went, they were cleansed. One of them, when he saw he was healed, came back, praising God in a loud voice. He threw himself at Jesus' feet and thanked him – and he was a Samaritan.** (NIV)

All ten were healed, but only one – only one said, "Thank you." As we make progress, we must remember to give *praise* to God for all that He does.

Prayer, promises, progress, praise – with those four P's in your pod, you can't go wrong.

Chapter 11
Where I've Been,
Where I Am, Where I'm Going

The first stage of my journey as a Christian began on October 4, 1959, in Log Cabin Baptist Church, Macon, GA, where I made my public profession of faith. For those of you unfamiliar with that term, "public profession of faith," means that I made the conscious decision to be a follower of Jesus. I accepted Christ's gift of salvation and made Him the Lord of my life. I walked down the aisle of my church during the invitational hymn and made this decision public. I was six years old at the time.

Some may feel that six is too young to make such a decision. Even though I didn't understand everything that was involved in my decision, I understood enough to know that God loved me and sent Jesus to die on the cross for my sins. I loved God enough to accept His Gift. From this humble beginning, my faith began to grow and mature.

Some people in my community of faith believed every question had a nice little pat answer, and there was a reason for everything that happened. There were no gray areas at all in life – just black or white, wrong or right. Oh, yes, and all of the rules applied to everyone with no exceptions. I was taught that people who didn't believe exactly the way our church taught were wrong and couldn't possibly be pleasing God. As I grew older, I never questioned any of these teachings and I allowed myself to be programmed to believe this way, too. I felt that God was lucky to have me on His team. I felt that if all Christians would be like me, the world would truly be a wonderful place – somewhat like the Garden of Eden before the fall.

By the time I reached high school, I was a Christian publican. I was holier-than-thou and I had absolutely no tolerance for anyone who dared to disagree with my religious beliefs. I had allowed myself to become consumed with other peoples' ideas and concepts of God. I was more concerned with what those people thought about me than what I thought about myself or, for that matter, what I thought about God or what He thought about me.

Over a period of time, I began to question some of the ideas that I had been taught. I began to realize that my beliefs were somewhat inconsistent.

For example, if God accepts us, as I had been taught and as the hymn implies, *Just as I am*, then why were some people shunned by the church because of the length of their hair or the clothes they wore?

That is just one example. There are many others. As a result of my questioning, I came face to face with reality-- I DID NOT HAVE A FAITH OF MY OWN. The faith I had was borrowed from other Christians and didn't fit me at all. It was as if I were playing dress-up in my mother's old clothes. I was no longer satisfied with my borrowed faith.

I was no longer holier-than-thou, but was scared and unsure of myself and my faith. I had no testimony anymore. I wasn't sure if I believed what I believed because I REALLY BELIEVED IT or just because someone TOLD me to believe it.

So began the second stage of my Christian journey....the stage that got me to where I am now. I read the Bible for the first time from cover to cover--and no, I didn't understand it all, but I did gain a few insights. For the first time the Word of God came alive to me. I realized that some of the verses I had previously been taught to justify certain beliefs had been taken out of context. I found out that you can prove/disprove anything you want using verses from the Bible.

I learned from the Scriptures beginning with Creation and continuing all through the struggles of the Israelites that all God wanted was to have a relationship with us. The entire message of the Bible points to God's love. A love that was so deep He (through Christ) would DIE for us. I discovered that no matter what I may encounter in life, God through Christ has already been there, whether it be physical pain or emotional pain.

I learned that Christianity is NOT a *one size fits all*, but rather *a size for everyone - quantities unlimited*. I realized that every person has to meet God where he/she is...and, praise God, He meets us on a personal, individual basis exactly where we are in life. He accepts us as we are and nurtures us from there.

Psalm 23:1a reads **The Lord is my Shepherd.** (KJV) The Lord is **my** caring, personal, feeling, understanding, Shepherd. That Shepherd has never been more real to me than He was on April 11, 1988. That was the day that Iris and I were returning from a weekend trip to Charleston, SC. I was driving. I swerved to miss another car and the next thing I knew I was completely out of control.

My initial thought was, "This can't be happening to me. I've swerved to miss things before so why can't I get the car back under control?"

I tried so hard to regain control of that car. I fought and I fought the wheel, but I could not regain control. It went from side to side, it did 360's, it left the pavement backward, it went up on its side and finally, after what seemed an eternity, came to rest on its roof.

Terror doesn't even come close to describing what I experienced and felt that day. Iris and I had talked to one another the entire time the car had been spinning, but I was still afraid to look at her for fear of what I might see. I was so afraid that I had injured her. But finally I did look and, thank God, there were no blood, no scratches. We were both still in one piece.

If I had a nickel for every time a well-meaning person told me that my wreck was God's Will and that He was trying to teach me something, I would be wealthy. And when I would ask, "Well, why did God include Iris in my lesson," I was quickly told by one that, "The innocent sometimes have to suffer for the guilty."

My reply to that is *baloney* (or bologna if you want to be formal). My God doesn't cause a car to careen out of control at 65 MPH to teach me or anyone else anything. No one will ever convince me it was "God's Will." I just can't picture God saying, "Well, there go Debi and Iris down the road. I've been meaning to teach Debi a lesson. Watch this, Son, while I scare her into shape."

No, I won't accept that. However, I can picture God saying something like this: "Son, Debi is about to lose control of that car. She needs us to help her through this.

Now hurry, let's get in that car with her and Iris. Hang on. Here we go!"

Well, if God didn't will it, then why? Why did that wreck happen? I don't know. I'm human, I lost control. It was simply an accident. Even though God didn't cause or allow that wreck to teach me anything, He has given me insight as a result of the wreck and I have learned and grown from the experience:

> I learned that I'm not perfect and it's okay. Prior to the accident I had a real problem accepting my mistakes. I always strove for perfection but I learned that I'm not perfect, I'm human! I don't have to be perfect.

> I learned that when I'm totally out of control, God is still in control. The wreck could have been much worse. I know God guided the car to land safely where it did.

> God didn't STOP the wreck from happening, but He was with us THROUGH it. Just like He is in life. Our problems do not disappear, but God is always with us and guides us through them.

> I learned that there doesn't have to be a reason or an explanation for everything that happens. I've come to realize that it's okay not to have an answer for everything. There wasn't a reason for my losing control of that car – it just happened.

So where am I now? I'm learning to accept myself for who I am, created in God's image. I'm learning to accept my limitations. I'm learning I don't always meet my goals.

God helped me begin understanding that lesson in Salem, MO, on my first mission trip. I have acrophobia, which is the fear of heights. However, while I was there I felt truly led by God to paint the cross – on top of the chapel porch. At first I think I told God if He wanted it painted, He could come down and do it Himself. But as the week progressed I became more and more aware that He wanted me to paint it. So, up the ladder I went with all of my church friends cheering me on. To say that I wasn't afraid would be a lie. I was scared silly and my knees were knocking the entire time. I was on the second rung from the top of the ladder (the highest I'd ever been in my life). I was able to paint the entire front of the cross; however, I couldn't reach the back of the cross from that position. I kept trying to WILL myself to climb to the next step to get on the roof but I just could not do it. I ended up climbing down the ladder without completing the job and Iris had to climb up and finish it for me. I was shocked and confused – after all, God wanted me to paint the cross – He TOLD me so. Why had I been so afraid? I suppose I thought God would miraculously take my fear away. I was extremely disappointed in myself. As I reflected on this that night in bed, 1 Corinthians 3:1-2 came to mind – **Brothers, I could not address you as spiritual but as worldly – mere infants in Christ. I gave you milk, not solid food, for you were not yet ready for it. Indeed, you are still not ready.** (NIV) I realized that we are all at different stages in our lives, as well as in our spiritual growth. Maybe one day I'll be able to climb on a roof without fear, or maybe I won't. The point is it doesn't matter; God loves me as I am.

I'm learning – that's me, a perpetual student – not to compare myself with other people. My response or reaction to a certain situation may not be the same as someone else's, but it doesn't make either of us wrong, just different. It's just like driving in London – they don't drive on the wrong side of the street, they drive on the <u>other</u> side of the street.

I understand that I don't have all the answers and at times make choices that aren't wise. I'm learning (God's not finished with me yet) it's okay to have times of confusion when the questions are there but the answers are not.

Well, that's where I've been and where I am, but where am I going? I don't know. I only know where I've been and where I am. But I do know one thing. Wherever I go, whatever I do, I have a caring, personal, feeling, understanding, accepting Shepherd going ahead of me, carrying me when necessary and guiding me along my way. And He and I will continue to dance in the garage of my life.

About the Author

Debi is the Founder and CEO of Attitude, Common Sense, Etc. Inc. – a company promoting the idea that we're at the helm of our life's journey and the route we take depends on how we steer our boat. She has been speaking to audiences most of her life, beginning in church and continuing in other venues. Her target audiences are schools, churches, civic groups and businesses. She will present an entertaining but inspiring message that will ignite the fire within that we have the power to make the right choices for our lives. We have the power to "steer our boat."

She is also celebrating her 34th year of Federal Civil Service and is currently employed by the U.S. Government Printing Office.

She has been a member of Toastmasters International since 1999 and served as Area 35 Governor for District 14 during 2003-2004. She attained her goal of DTM (Distinguished Toastmaster) in June 2005.

Debi is a member of Due West United Methodist Church in Marietta, Georgia.

She enjoys playing with her grandchildren, reading, writing, music, stamping (greeting cards), hiking, computer games, Sudoku puzzles, swimming, and watching her beloved Atlanta Braves and Georgia Bulldogs.

She is passionate about personal responsibility, utilizing common sense and common courtesy, being good stewards of the tax dollar, and living by a high standard of integrity. She has participated in several Habitat for Humanity builds and Breast Cancer Walks.

Debi was born in Macon, GA; grew up in Hanahan, SC (near Charleston); and returned to Georgia (Marietta) in 1983, where she currently lives with her husband, Matthew, two dogs, and a cat. She and Matthew have three grown children and two granddaughters.